Praise for
THE ANATOMY OF PEACE

"I love this book. Having read it, the circumstances I encounter every day seem different to me—whether in sports, business, or family life, the ideas apply to every facet of life. I can't wait to share this book and its concepts with others."

DANNY AINGE, GENERAL MANAGER, THE BOSTON CELTICS

"Having been intensely involved in peacemaking, I can honestly say that this is a significant and important book that lays out innovative strategies for building sustainable peace."

**URI SAVIR, PRESIDENT, THE PERES CENTER FOR PEACE,
TEL-AVIV, AND FORMER DIRECTOR GENERAL,
ISRAEL MINISTRY OF FOREIGN AFFAIRS**

"After years of applying these ideas with youth and their parents, I can say that this is powerful medicine for the soul. These ideas change hearts, heal deep wounds, and bring parents and children together."

**MIKE MERCHANT, PRESIDENT AND CHIEF EXECUTIVE OFFICER,
ANASAZI FOUNDATION**

"*The Anatomy of Peace*, a truly inspirational book, could change the face of humanity. The world would be a dramatically better place if even a few of us would be guided by its powerful ideas. *The Anatomy of Peace* should be required reading—for everyone."

**MARION BLUMENTHAL LAZAN, HOLOCAUST SURVIVOR,
COAUTHOR OF *FOUR PERFECT PEBBLES***

"A powerful work that has a profound impact on all things personal and professional. It illustrates that the path to peace and to the resolution of our most troubling conflicts requires not only different actions but a different way of being. Even better, it shows you how to get there. It is a book I will share widely and return to again and again."

**LAURA WHITWORTH, COFOUNDER, THE BIGGER GAME COMPANY
AND THE COACHES TRAINING INSTITUTE**

"A stunning work of wisdom and insight.... Everyone, from neighbors to the heads of nations, ought to read and live the teachings of this book."

KENT MURDOCK, PRESIDENT AND CEO, O.C. TANNER

"*The Anatomy of Peace* is one of those rare works that somehow finds its way into the heart. Before you know it you will be emotionally invested in the same process as the characters in this story. Be prepared to be at once challenged, moved, and called forth to become the person you know you should be."

MIKE BUNDRANT, PUBLISHER, *HEALTHY TIMES NEWSPAPER*

"Profound in depth yet simple in message—an astounding work of immense impact, both personally and professionally. This is the next major lever in terms of how organizations improve performance."

NICK JESSETT, PROGRAMME MANAGER, ROLLS-ROYCE

"I can't begin to explain how much I love *The Anatomy of Peace*. It goes twenty times deeper than *Leadership and Self-Deception* in the same amount of space. It's an amazing, inspiring book that has opened up new ways for me to think about my life. I look forward to reading it again and again! I can't recommend it more highly!"

DAREN CONNEL, CEO, COMMUNICATE WIRELESS

"A true masterpiece with far-reaching implications. I couldn't put it down."

NAN O'CONNOR, MASTER CERTIFIED COACH

"Simply phenomenal. Arresting. Words escape me. *The Anatomy of Peace* is a tremendous resource for people who are looking to improve their quality of life."

MURALI IYER, VICE PRESIDENT AND MANAGING DIRECTOR, THE REVERE GROUP

"*The Anatomy of Peace* is an emotionally moving and fascinating work with the potential to have a profound global impact, one person at a time. It has me thinking new and deep thoughts—about myself, about others, and about problems we are facing in our communities and around the world."

JOHN NICHOLS, PRESIDENT,
DISABILITY RESOURCE GROUP, INC.

"This book is a joy to the jaded. It gets beneath highly regarded behavioral theses and shows how change in behavior is not enough. A simple tale, quietly told without condescension, it shows the potential and strength of our ordinary humanity. I feel I have grown from inside by reading it. The book helps people to know their neighbor without fear. And that is about as good as it gets."

STEPHEN PRYOR, VICE CHAIR, GRUBB INSTITUTE
FOR BEHAVIORAL STUDIES (LONDON),
FORMER ENGLISH PRISON SERVICE GOVERNOR

"*The Anatomy of Peace* is a brilliant work that takes Arbinger's concepts to a new level and applies them to all areas of our lives. The book has true everyman appeal, as everyone will see themselves in the book's story. The takeaway is huge: no matter our circumstances, we always retain the choice of being at peace."

SCOTT DUGAN, PRESIDENT AND CEO, MID-PLAINS CENTER

"A deep and insightful book! It is an extremely powerful tool for shifting individuals to a new space and dimension where solutions can be found and applied to challenges facing most people in the world today."

VINDRA NAIPAUL, CEO, XTRA FOODS,
TRINIDAD AND TOBAGO

"Reading *The Anatomy of Peace* is truly a *wow* experience. The book offers a way out of conflict that relies on my choices. How incredibly empowering! It is an extraordinary book that will help you find peace in any situation. It has changed the way I look at life."

SISTER MAUREEN FITZGERALD, ASCJ, DEAN OF
ADMISSIONS AND ACADEMICS, COR JESU ACADEMY

"Nothing I can write will do justice to this work. I have used these ideas professionally to resolve organizational conflicts that threatened to shut down a contractor operating a Navy base and to diffuse grievances from disgruntled employees determined to rid themselves of their managers. In each instance, disasters were averted and hearts of war were turned to hearts of peace. If the world were to read and adopt the principles contained in this book, my profession would be a relic of the past."

RUSSELL PENDERGRASS, CAPTAIN, UNITED STATES NAVY

"*The Anatomy of Peace* is a moving, powerful, wonderful book. It awakened me to the need to look more intentionally inside my heart. As much as I want peace in the world, it must start with my own deep understanding of why I sometimes create my own little wars or participate in others."

PATRICK WILLIAMS, EDD, MCC, CEO AND FOUNDER,
INSTITUTE FOR LIFE COACH TRAINING

"Inspiring and thrilling! Once you start reading it, you can't put it down. The story is beautiful because it's so real. The book doesn't lecture but rather invites the reader into an experience of profound learning. I immediately saw myself in the characters and learned as they learned. Thank you for this inspiration! It has filled me with a passion for peace, both inside and out."

ECE SIRIN, COFOUNDER, BEE CONSULTING, ISTANBUL, TURKEY

"This is a masterful and important work that shows how we blame others for problems we ourselves have created. It gently leads the reader to take a hard look in the mirror."

SCOTT BARTON, SENIOR VICE PRESIDENT, CAPITAL ONE

"*The Anatomy of Peace* takes the reader to a deeper level of understanding of the Arbinger material. It has opened my eyes to how my heart has been at war. I feel a renewed commitment to continually examine my way of being. I can only say bravo and thank you!"

SUSAN VALDISERRI, CPCC, PCC,
PROFESSIONAL AND EXECUTIVE COACH

"Parents and children, brothers and sisters, liberals and conservatives, blacks and whites, Irish Catholics and Irish Protestants, Muslims and Christians; what a better world this would be if only we would read and apply the teachings of this book!"

GARY DYER, CEO,
FARM CREDIT SERVICES SOUTHWEST

"Excellent! Even better than *Leadership and Self-Deception*. A book with tremendous power to change perceptions and lives. As you read it, you will not only be rethinking many of your assumptions about life but also wanting to make positive changes right away in relationships you have, both personally and professionally."

ELLIOT SAINER, CEO, ASPEN EDUCATION GROUP, INC.

"Powerful! I am a better person for having read this book. I felt compelled to see myself more clearly and then enabled to resolve conflicts in my relationships. I'm excited to see how far I can extend the influence of these truths in my life."

RICH ANDERSON, MARKETING COMMUNICATIONS MANAGER,
TAHITIAN NONI CAFE

"I still have goose bumps from the thrill of reading this beautiful book. An easy and compelling read, it is a rare book that has equal application personally and globally. At the same time that it powerfully and poignantly points to solutions for problems as deep as those in the Middle East, it delivers a deeply personal message that awakens new hope, motivation, and commitment toward inward peace. It has empowered me to improve every relationship—at home, at work, and in the political sphere. Thank you!"

MARK SHURTLEFF, UTAH ATTORNEY GENERAL

"The theoretical work underlying this book is deep and significant in its diagnosis of the ills of our society—from the small scale of individual self-deceptions to self-deceptions of whole cultures."

ROM HARRÉ, PROFESSOR OF PSYCHOLOGY, FELLOW EMERITUS, LINACRE COLLEGE, OXFORD UNIVERSITY

"A book all human beings can relate to, lighting up flashbulbs every few pages. The simplicity of the story is a vehicle for a deep philosophy to positive relationships, starting at the family, reaching out to the larger community, and relevant to all creeds and cultures. An empathic understanding of others is the cornerstone to a peaceful world."

ROSALIND PORTMAN, COFOUNDER, FAMILY LINKS UK

"I love this book. It is a dramatic and deeply penetrating look at how to achieve peace in one's heart and then how to extend it to others, even under the most difficult circumstances. It is an extremely powerful work—better than I can express."

MICHAEL MARCHESE, COO, GRAND CANYON COUNCIL, BOY SCOUTS OF AMERICA

"An impressively clear expression of a solution for peace. How different our world would look if we were willing to practice and integrate these concepts in our lives."

MARJOLEIN HINS, MANAGING DIRECTOR, Q-SEARCH, THE NETHERLANDS

"Great, great read with powerful insights into how our personal choices preload us for war or peace in all of our relationships."

TOM LEONARD, GROUP CHAIR, VISTAGE INTERNATIONAL

"A clear and moving account of how issues relating to race, religion, and color can become perverted by the overpowering need for justification, and how this need is at the heart of war itself—both internal and external. An absolute must read."

ISHAK BIN ISMAIL, SINGAPORE

"This beautiful book reminds us that the foundation of a happy, peaceful life is compassion and humanity and reveals how our hearts may be at war in everyday relationships at home or work. It challenges us to use this insight for active and continuous change. It should be on the curriculum for all caring professions and studied by all leaders who want to create effective teams."

JANET SAUNDERS, MATRON, ROYAL UNITED HOSPITAL, BATH UK

"An intriguing book that provides the tools for transcending differences between people. I believe and hope that it will help people to see the divinity in others, even when it is difficult to do so—a profoundly important message that resonates deeply within me."

TODD CROWE, AIA, PC, CROWE ARCHITECTS

"*The Anatomy of Peace* lights us up in two places: the heart and the world. For the first time the dots have been connected between inner heartfelt peace and outer world peace . . . and in this entertaining novel, full of lively dialogue, the connection is a thrill."

STEVE CHANDLER, AUTHOR OF *THE STORY OF YOU*

"This book is powerful. It not only identifies the problem but presents clear and workable solutions for challenges at work, at home, and in the community. It is an empowering book that will change the lives of all who read it."

STEWART HUGHES, CEO, UNICITY INTERNATIONAL

"*The Anatomy of Peace* is truly transforming and powerful material. Arbinger has taken the burden out of leading in our organization by teaching us to truly care about our colleagues and individually take responsibility for creating a powerful organization, which will ultimately transform the level of care that we can provide to our clients."

DON SERRATT, FOUNDER AND CEO, LIFE WORKS, UK

"Reading this book is an extraordinary experience. It shows how to become an agent of peace—at home, at work, and in the world. This is an important book and a service to mankind."

"Having finished this book and absorbed the wise words that fill every page, I wonder why we teach mathematics to enforce logical thinking, languages for intercultural communication, and so on, but we lack the essence: a proper method for social behaviour! I say let schools and universities offer courses designed by the Arbinger Institute, train politicians and statesmen in *The Anatomy of Peace,* and invite Arbinger to train all kinds of people in the understanding of their very own contribution to the advancement of peace in the world!"

"A penetrating and dramatically moving book that unearths how we go to war against others in our hearts and deny their humanity through self-justifying views and behaviors. It makes me weep with recognition and hope."

"To adopt the essence of this book is the true road map for peace."

"On a personal level, I found many examples of how I was looking at people wrongly and, by doing so, was treating them wrongly. On a more global level, I could apply these lessons to any international conflict seen on CNN and see how this process can be used to end age-old conflicts that have plagued society for many years."

"Delivers some powerful insights...No matter whom you wish to change your relationship with—your child, parent, friend, or colleague—this book can help you identify problematic behavior and show you a way to better relate to others. It warrants a place in the library of those who seek to advance the cause of reconciliation and peace."

—THE WORLD & I, A PUBLICATION OF
THE UNIVERSAL PEACE FEDERATION

"Offers specific tools that can be used any time a defensive reaction to an offense or an injustice springs up... *The Anatomy of Peace* is at once a challenge, an invitation, and a way through to a place of peace inside all of us that is not only attainable but the very nature of who we are."

—SHIFT, THE MAGAZINE OF THE INSTITUTE OF NOETIC SCIENCES

"Offers a realistic portrayal of conflict and is prescriptive without being preachy. It is difficult to read *The Anatomy of Peace* and not recognize the role we all play in perpetuating conflict. One can't help but fantasize that, somehow, the book could become required reading for world leaders."

—GREATER GOOD MAGAZINE

"Rarely have I read anything that held my attention the way this book did. To find that kind of reading experience in the context of a book that covers such disparate topics as parenting, managing employees, Middle East peace, and self-actualization is truly astonishing."

—JO ELLEN GREEN KAISER, SENIOR EDITOR, ZEEK

"Phenomenal...compelling...vivid...poignant. This is a book that every manager, teacher, advisor, and parent should read and apply."

—STEVEN C. WHEELWRIGHT, PROFESSOR EMERITUS,
HARVARD BUSINESS SCHOOL

"*The Anatomy of Peace* is a brilliantly written, stimulating read with a rare clarity that awakens reflection and compels action. I recommend it without hesitation to anyone interested in finding solutions to conflicts ranging from the personal to the global."

—GILEAD SHER, FORMER CHIEF OF STAFF OF THE PRIME MINISTER OF ISRAEL AND CHIEF NEGOTIATOR WITH THE PALESTINIANS

"*The Anatomy of Peace* is more than just a book to read or an idea to consider, it is a life raft for the countless many who are suffering in silence and drowning in fear."

—IYANLA VANZANT, AUTHOR, LIFE COACH, AND FOUNDER OF THE INNER VISIONS INSTITUTE FOR SPIRITUAL DEVELOPMENT

The
Anatomy
of PEACE

The
Anatomy
of PEACE

•

RESOLVING THE
HEART OF CONFLICT

The Arbinger Institute

Berrett–Koehler Publishers, Inc.
San Francisco
a BK Life book

Berrett-Koehler Publishers, Inc.
235 Montgomery Street, Suite 650
San Francisco, CA 94104-2916
Tel: (415) 288-0260   Fax: (415) 362-2512   www.bkconnection.com

Ordering Information
Quantity sales. Special discounts are available on quantity purchases by corporations, associations, and others. For details, contact the "Special Sales Department" at the Berrett-Koehler address above.

Individual sales. Berrett-Koehler publications are available through most bookstores. They can also be ordered directly from Berrett-Koehler: Tel: (800) 929-2929; Fax: (802) 864-7626; www.bkconnection.com.

Orders for college textbook/course adoption use. Please contact Berrett-Koehler: Tel: (800) 929-2929; Fax: (802) 864-7626.

Orders by U.S. trade bookstores and wholesalers. Please contact Ingram Publisher Services, Tel: (800) 509-4887; Fax: (800) 838-1149; E-mail: customer.service@ingrampublisherservices.com; or visit www.ingrampublisherservices.com/Ordering for details about electronic ordering.

Berrett-Koehler and the BK logo are registered trademarks of Berrett-Koehler Publishers, Inc.

Printed in the United States of America

Berrett-Koehler books are printed on long-lasting acid-free paper. When it is available, we choose paper that has been manufactured by environmentally responsible processes. These may include using trees grown in sustainable forests, incorporating recycled paper, minimizing chlorine in bleaching, or recycling the energy produced at the paper mill.

Library of Congress Cataloging-in-Publication Data
The anatomy of peace : resolving the heart of conflict / by the Arbinger Institute.
    p. cm.
  Includes index.
  ISBN: 978-1-57675-334-7 (hardcover)
  ISBN: 978-1-57675-584-6 (pbk.)
    1. Conflict management.   2. Interpersonal conflict.   3. Peace—Psychological aspects. I. Arbinger Institute.
HM1126.A53. 2006
303.6'9—dc22   2006040079

FIRST EDITION
15 14   15

Copyediting and proofreading by PeopleSpeak.
Book design and composition by Beverly Butterfield, Girl of the West Productions.
Indexing by Rachel Rice.

Our fate is shaped from within

ourselves outward, never

from without inward.

JACQUES LUSSEYRAN

Contents

Part IV Spreading Peace

Preface

Typically we assume that people who are in conflict want solutions. And they do, of course. Parents of belligerent children want the belligerence to end. Those who work for tyrannical managers want an end to the tyranny. Citizens of weakened nations want to be treated with respect. And so on. People want solutions. But notice that the preferred solution in each case is that others change. Should we be surprised, then, when conflicts linger and problems remain?

What if in our conflicts with others there is something we want more than solutions? What if conflicts at home, conflicts at work, and conflicts in the world stem from the same root cause? And what if, individually and collectively, we systematically misunderstand that cause and unwittingly perpetuate the very problems we think we are trying to solve? These are among the important questions explored in *The Anatomy of Peace*.

Through an intriguing story of parents struggling with their children and with problems that have come to consume their lives, we learn from once-bitter enemies the way to find peace whenever war is upon us. Yusuf al-Falah, an Arab, and Avi Rozen, a Jew, each lost his father at the hands of the other's ethnic cousins. *The Anatomy of Peace* is the story of how they came together, how they help warring parents and children to come together, and how we too can find our way out of the struggles that weigh us down.

"But home, workplace, and world conflicts are entirely different issues," you might say. "Few families and companies in the world do internal battle with artillery and tanks."

True enough. But not all weapons are aimed at the flesh. Look around. Home and workplace casualties are everywhere. Bitterness, envy, indifference, resentment—these are hallmarks of the hot and cold wars that fester in the hearts of family members, neighbors, colleagues, and former friends the world over. If we can't find the way to peace in these relationships, what hope have we for finding it between nations at war?

For those who have not read our prior book, *Leadership and Self-Deception*, *The Anatomy of Peace* stands on its own as a thought-provoking exploration of a body of ideas that points the way to peace in all of our interactions. Those who have read *Leadership and Self-Deception* know about the issue of self-deception (the problem of not knowing one has a problem) and how it affects all other problems. They will not be surprised, therefore, to encounter some of the same ideas in *The Anatomy of Peace* and to learn how those issues play a pivotal role in conflict situations at home, at work, and between countries throughout the world. They will also recognize one of the key characters from *Leadership and Self-Deception*, Lou Herbert, as *The Anatomy of Peace* takes the reader back in time to when Lou first learned the ideas that ultimately transformed his family life and his company.

While *Leadership and Self-Deception* focused on the workplace, *The Anatomy of Peace* explores the freeing and surprising implications of these ideas in all aspects of life. In addition, while *Leadership and Self-Deception* explored how to solve self-deception in oneself, *The Anatomy of Peace* goes beyond, exploring how to spread that solution among others.

Although some of the stories in this book were inspired by actual events, no character or organization described in this book represents any specific person or organization. In many respects, these characters are each of us. They share our strengths and our weaknesses, our aspiration and our despair. They are seeking solutions to problems that weigh us down. They are us, and we are them. So their lessons offer us hope.

Hope? Yes. Because our problems, as theirs, are not what they seem. This is at once our challenge and our opportunity.

PART I

The Heart of Peace

1 · Enemies in the Desert

"I'm not going!" The teenage girl's shriek pulled everyone's attention to her. "You can't make me go!"

The woman she was yelling at attempted a reply. "Jenny, listen to me."

"I'm not going!" Jenny screamed. "I don't care what you say. I won't!"

At this, the girl turned and faced a middle-aged man who seemed torn between taking her into his arms and slinking away unnoticed. "Daddy, please!" she bawled.

Lou Herbert, who was watching the scene from across the parking lot, knew before Jenny spoke that this was her father. He could see himself in the man. He recognized the ambivalence he felt toward his own child, eighteen-year-old Cory, who was standing stiffly at his side.

Cory had recently spent a year in prison for a drug conviction. Less than three months after his release, he was arrested for stealing a thousand dollars' worth of prescription painkillers, bringing more shame upon himself and, Lou thought, the family. *This treatment program better do something to shape Cory up*, Lou said to himself. He looked back at Jenny and her father, whom she was now clutching in desperation. Lou was glad Cory had been sent here by court order. It meant that a stunt like Jenny's would earn Cory another stint in jail. Lou was pretty sure their morning would pass without incident.

"Lou, over here."

Carol, Lou's wife, was motioning for him to join her. He tugged at Cory's arm. "Come on, your mom wants us."

"Lou, this is Yusuf al-Falah," she said, introducing the man standing next to her. "Mr. al-Falah's the one who's been helping us get everything arranged for Cory."

"Of course," Lou said, forcing a smile.

Yusuf al-Falah was the Arab half of an odd partnership in the Arizona desert. An immigrant from Jerusalem by way of Jordan in the 1960s, he came to the United States to further his education and ended up staying, eventually becoming a professor of education at Arizona State University. In the summer of 1978, he befriended a young and bitter Israeli man, Avi Rozen, who had come to the States following the death of his father in the Yom Kippur War of 1973. At the time, Avi was flunking out of school. In an experimental program, he and others struggling with their grades were given a chance to rehabilitate their college careers and transcripts during a long summer in the high mountains and deserts of Arizona. Al-Falah, Rozen's elder by fifteen years, led the program.

It was a forty-day course in survival, the kind of experience Arabs and Israelis of al-Falah and Rozen's era had been steeped in from their youth. Over those forty days, the two men made a connection. Muslim and Jewish, both regarded land—sometimes the very same land—as sacred. Out of this shared respect for the soil gradually grew a respect for each other, despite their differences in belief and the strife that divided their people.

Or so Lou had been told.

In truth, Lou was skeptical of the happy face that had been painted on the relationship between al-Falah and Rozen. To him it smelled like PR, a game Lou knew from his own corporate marketing experience. *Come be healed by two former ene-*

mies who now raise their families together in peace. The more he thought about the al-Falah/Rozen story, the less he believed it.

If he had examined himself at that moment, Lou would have been forced to admit that it was precisely this Middle Eastern intrigue surrounding Camp Moriah, as it was called, that had lured him onto the plane with Carol and Cory. Certainly he had every reason not to come. Five executives had recently left his company, putting the organization in peril. If he had to spend two days away, which al-Falah and Rozen were requiring, he needed to unwind on a golf course or near a pool, not commiserate with a group of despairing parents.

"Thank you for helping us," he said to al-Falah, feigning gratitude. He continued watching the girl out of the corner of his eye. She was still shrieking between sobs and both clinging to and clawing at her father. "Looks like you have your hands full here."

Al-Falah's eyes creased in a smile. "I suppose we do. Parents can become a bit hysterical on occasions like this."

Parents? Lou thought. *The girl is the one in hysterics.* But al-Falah had struck up a conversation with Cory before Lou could point this out to him.

"You must be Cory."

"That would be me," Cory said flippantly. Lou registered his disapproval by digging his fingers into Cory's bicep. Cory flexed in response.

"I'm glad to meet you, Son," al-Falah said, taking no notice of Cory's tone. "I've been looking forward to it." Leaning in, he added, "No doubt more than you have. I can't imagine you're very excited to be here."

Cory didn't respond immediately. "Not really. No," he finally said, pulling his arm out of his father's grasp. He reflexively brushed his arm, as if to dust off any molecular fibers that might have remained from his father's grip.

"Don't blame you," al-Falah said as he looked at Lou and then back at Cory. "Don't blame you a bit. But you know something?" Cory looked at him warily. "I'd be surprised if you feel that way for long. You might. But I'd be surprised." He patted Cory on the back. "I'm just glad you're here, Cory."

"Yeah, okay," Cory said less briskly than before. Then, back to form, he chirped, "Whatever you say."

Lou shot Cory an angry look.

"So, Lou," al-Falah said, "you're probably not too excited about being here either, are you?"

"On the contrary," Lou said, forcing a smile. "We're quite happy to be here."

Carol, standing beside him, knew that wasn't at all true. But he had come. She had to give him that. He often complained about inconveniences, but in the end he most often made the inconvenient choice. She reminded herself to stay focused on this positive fact—on the good that lay not too far beneath the surface.

"We're glad you're here, Lou," al-Falah answered. Turning to Carol, he added, "We know what it means for a mother to leave her child in the hands of another. It is an honor that you would give us the privilege."

"Thank you, Mr. al-Falah," Carol said. "It means a lot to hear you say that."

"Well, it's how we feel," he responded. "And please, call me Yusuf. You too Cory," he said, turning in Cory's direction. "In fact, *especially* you. Please call me Yusuf. Or 'Yusi,' if you want. That's what most of the youngsters call me."

In place of the cocksure sarcasm he had exhibited so far, Cory simply nodded.

A few minutes later, Carol and Lou watched as Cory loaded into a van with the others who would be spending the next sixty days in the wilderness. All, that is, except for the girl Jenny, who, when she realized her father wouldn't be rescuing her, ran across the street and sat belligerently on a concrete wall. Lou noticed she wasn't wearing anything on her feet. He looked skyward at the morning Arizona sun. *She'll have some sense burned into her before long,* he thought.

Jenny's parents seemed lost as to what to do. Lou saw Yusuf go over to them, and a couple of minutes later the parents went into the building, glancing back one last time at their daughter. Jenny howled as they stepped through the doors and out of her sight.

Lou and Carol milled about the parking lot with a few of the other parents, engaging in small talk. They visited with a man named Pettis Murray from Dallas, Texas, a couple named Lopez from Corvallis, Oregon, and a woman named Elizabeth Wingfield from London, England. Mrs. Wingfield was currently living in Berkeley, California, where her husband was a visiting professor in Middle Eastern studies. Like Lou, her attraction to Camp Moriah was mostly due to her curiosity about the founders and their history. She was only reluctantly accompanying her nephew, whose parents couldn't afford the trip from England.

Carol made a remark about it being a geographically diverse group, and though everyone nodded and smiled, it was obvious that these conversations were barely registering. Most of the parents were preoccupied with their kids in the van and cast furtive glances in their direction every minute or so. For Lou's part, he was most interested in why nobody seemed to be doing anything about Jenny.

Lou was about to ask Yusuf what he was going to do so that the vehicle could set out to take their children to the trail. Just then, however, Yusuf patted the man he was talking to on the back and began to walk toward the street. Jenny didn't acknowledge him.

"Jenny," he called out to her. "Are you alright?"

"What do you think?" she shrieked back. "You can't make me go, you can't!"

"You're right, Jenny, we can't. And we wouldn't. Whether you go will be up to you."

Lou turned to the van hoping Cory hadn't heard this. *Maybe you can't make him go, Yusi,* he thought, *but I can. And so can the court.*

Yusuf didn't say anything for a minute. He just stood there, looking across the street at the girl while cars occasionally passed between them. "Would you mind if I came over, Jenny?" he finally called.

She didn't say anything.

"I'll just come over and we can talk."

Yusuf crossed the street and sat down on the sidewalk. Lou strained to hear what they were saying but couldn't for the distance and traffic.

"Okay, it's about time to get started everyone."

Lou turned toward the voice. A short youngish-looking man with a bit of a paunch stood at the doorway to the building, beaming what Lou thought was an overdone smile. He had a thick head of hair that made him look younger than he was. "Come on in, if you would," he said. "We should probably be getting started."

"What about our kids?" Lou protested, pointing at the idling vehicle.

"They'll be leaving shortly, I'm sure," the man responded. "You've had a chance to say good-bye, haven't you?"

They all nodded.

"Good. Then this way, if you please."

Lou took a last look at the vehicle. Cory was staring straight ahead, apparently paying no attention to them. Carol was crying and waving at him anyway as the parents shuffled through the door.

"Avi Rozen," said the bushy-haired man as he extended his hand to Lou.

"Lou and Carol Herbert," Lou replied in the perfunctory tone he used with those who worked for him.

"Pleasure to meet you, Lou. Welcome, Carol," Avi said with an encouraging nod.

They filed through the door with the others and went up the stairs. This was to be their home for the next two days. *Two days during which we better learn what they're going to do to fix our son,* Lou thought.

2 · Deeper Matters

Lou looked around the room. Ten or so chairs were arranged in a U shape. Lou sat in the first of these. Jenny's father and mother were sitting across from him. The mother's face was drawn tight with worry. Blotchy red patches covered the skin on her neck and stretched across her face. The father was staring vacantly at the ground.

Behind them, Elizabeth Wingfield (a bit overdressed, Lou thought, in a chic business suit) was helping herself to a cup of tea at the bar against the far wall of the room.

Meanwhile, Pettis Murray, the fellow from Dallas, was taking his seat about halfway around the semicircle to Lou's right. He seemed pretty sharp to Lou, with the air of an executive—head high, jaw set, guarded.

The couple just to the other side of Pettis couldn't have been more in contrast. Miguel Lopez was an enormous man, with tattoos covering almost every square inch of his bare arms. He wore a beard and mustache so full that a black bandana tied tightly around his head was the only thing that kept his face from being completely obscured by hair. By contrast, his wife, Ria, was barely over five feet tall with a slender build. In the parking lot, she had been the most talkative of the group, while Miguel had mostly stood by in silence. Ria now nodded at Lou, the corners of her mouth hinting at a smile. He tipped his head toward her in acknowledgment and then continued scanning the room.

In the back, keeping to herself, was a person Lou hadn't yet met—an African American woman he guessed to be somewhere in her midforties. Unlike the others with children in the program, she had not been outside to see them off. Lou wondered whether she had brought a child, worked for Camp Moriah, or had some other reason for being there.

Lou turned to the front of the room, arms folded loosely across his chest. One thing he hated was wasting time, and it seemed they had been doing nothing but that since they'd arrived.

"Thank you all for coming," Avi said as he walked to the front. "I've been looking forward to meeting you in person and to getting to know your children. First of all, I know you're concerned about them—Teri and Carl, you especially," he said, glancing for a moment over at Jenny's parents. "Your presence here is a testament to your love for your children. You needn't trouble yourself about them. They will be well taken care of.

"In fact," he said after a brief pause, "they are not my primary concern."

"Who is, then?" Ria asked.

"You are, Ria. All of you."

"We are?" Lou repeated in surprise.

"Yes," Avi smiled.

Lou was never one to back down from a perceived challenge. In Vietnam he had served as a sergeant in the Marine Corps, and the gruesome experience had both hardened and sharpened him. His men referred to him as Hell-fire Herbert, a name that reflected both his loud, brash nature and his consequences-be-damned devotion to his unit. His men both feared and revered him: for most of them, he was the last person on earth they would want to spend a holiday with, but no other leader in the Marines brought more men back alive.

"And why are we your primary concern?" Lou asked pointedly.

"Because you don't think you should be," Avi answered.

Lou laughed politely. "That's a bit circular, isn't it?"

The others in the group, like spectators at a tennis match, looked back at Avi, anticipating his reply.

Avi smiled and looked down at the ground for a moment, thinking. "Tell us about Cory, Lou," he said finally. "What's he like?"

"Cory?"

"Yes."

"He is a boy with great talent who is wasting his life," Lou answered matter-of-factly.

"But he's a wonderful boy," Carol interjected, glancing warily at Lou. "He's made some mistakes, but he's basically a good kid."

"'Good kid'?" Lou scoffed, losing his air of nonchalance. "He's a *felon* for heaven's sake—twice over! Sure he has the ability to be good, but mere potential doesn't make him good. We wouldn't be here if he was such a good kid."

Carol bit her lip, and the other parents in the room fidgeted uncomfortably.

Sensing the discomfort around him, Lou leaned forward and added, "Sorry to speak so plainly, but I'm not here to celebrate my child's achievements. Frankly, I'm royally pissed at him."

"Leave the royalty to me, if you don't mind," Mrs. Wingfield quipped. She was seated two chairs to Lou's right, on the other side of Carol.

"Certainly," he said with a smile. "My apologies to the crown."

She tipped her head at him.

It was a light moment that all in the room could throw themselves into heavily, as heaviness was what had characterized too
much of their recent lives.

"Lou is quite right," Avi said after the moment had passed.
"We are here not because our children have been choosing well
but because they have been choosing poorly."

"That's what I'm saying," Lou nodded in agreement.

Avi smiled. "So what, then, is the solution? How can the
problems you are experiencing in your families be improved?"

"I should think that's obvious," Lou answered directly. "We
are here because our children have problems. And Camp
Moriah is in the business of helping children overcome their
problems. Isn't that right?"

Carol bristled at Lou's tone. He was now speaking in his
boardroom voice—direct, challenging, and abrasive. He rarely
took this tone with her, but it had become the voice of his interactions with Cory over the last few years. Carol couldn't remember the last time Lou and Cory had had an actual conversation.
When they spoke, it was a kind of verbal wrestling match, each
of them trying to anticipate the other's moves, searching for
weaknesses they could then exploit to force the other into sub-
mission. With no actual mat into which to press the other's flesh,
these verbal matches always ended in a draw: each of them
claimed hollow victory while living with ongoing defeat. She
silently called heavenward for help, as she had been taught to do
by her churchgoing parents. She wasn't sure there was a heaven
or any help to be had, but she broadcast her need all the same.

Avi smiled good-naturedly. "So Lou," he said, "Cory is a
problem. That's what you're saying."

"Yes."

"He needs to be fixed in some way—changed, motivated,
disciplined, corrected."

"Absolutely."

"And you've tried that?"

"Tried what?"

"Changing him."

"Of course."

"And has it worked? Has he changed?"

"Not yet, but that's why we're here. One day, no matter how hard a skull he has, he's going to get it. One way or the other."

"Maybe," Avi said without conviction.

"You don't think your program will work?" Lou asked, incredulously.

"That depends."

"On what?"

"On you."

Lou grunted. "How can the success of your program depend on me when you're the ones who will be working with my son over the coming two months?"

"Because you will be living with him over all the months afterward," Avi answered. "We can help, but if your family environment is the same when he gets home as it was when he left, whatever good happens here is unlikely to make much of a difference later. Yusuf and I are only temporary surrogates. You and Carol, all of you with your respective children," he said, motioning to the group, "are the helpers who matter."

Great, Lou thought. *A waste of time.*

"You said you want Cory to change," came a voice from the back, yanking Lou from his thoughts. It was Yusuf, who had finally joined the group.

"Yes," Lou answered.

"Don't blame you," Yusuf said. "But if that is what you want, there is something you need to know."

"What's that?"

"If you are going to invite change in him, there is something that first must change in you."

"Oh yeah?" Lou challenged. "And what would that be?"

Yusuf walked to the whiteboard that covered nearly the entire front wall of the room. "Let me draw something for you," he said.

THE CHANGE PYRAMID

"By the end of the day tomorrow," Yusuf said, turning to face the group, "we will have formulated a detailed strategy for helping others to change. That strategy will be illustrated by a diagram we call the Change Pyramid. We aren't yet ready to consider the pyramid in detail, so I've drawn only its basic structure. This overall structure will help us to discover a fundamental change that must occur in us if we are going to invite change in others."

"Okay, I'll bite," Lou said. "*What* fundamental change?"

"Look at the two areas in the pyramid," Yusuf invited. "Notice that the largest area by far is what I have labeled 'Helping things go right.' In comparison, the 'Dealing with things that are going wrong' area is tiny."

"Okay," Lou said, wondering what significance this had.

Yusuf continued. "The pyramid suggests that we should spend much more time and effort helping things go right than dealing with things that are going wrong. Unfortunately, however, these allocations of time and effort are typically reversed. We spend most of our time with others dealing with things that are going wrong. We try fixing our children, changing our spouses, correcting our employees, and disciplining those who aren't acting as we'd like. And when we're not actually *doing* these things, we're *thinking* about doing them or *worrying* about doing them. Am I right?" Yusuf looked around the room for a response.

"For example, Lou," he said, "would it be fair to say that you spend much of your time with Cory criticizing and challenging him?"

Lou thought about it. This was no doubt true in his case, but he didn't want to admit to it so easily.

"Yes, I'd say that's true," Carol admitted for him.

"Thanks," Lou mumbled under his breath. Carol looked straight ahead.

"It's certainly far too true of me as well," Yusuf said, coming to Lou's rescue. "It's only natural when confronting a problem that we try to correct it. Trouble is, when working with people, this hardly ever helps. Further correction rarely helps a child who is pouting, for example, or a spouse who is brooding, or a coworker who is blaming. In other words, most problems in life are not solved merely by correction."

"So what do you suggest?" Lou asked. "If your child was into drugs, what would you do, Yusuf? Just ignore it? Are you saying you shouldn't try to change him?"

"Maybe we should begin with a less extreme situation," Yusuf answered.

"Less extreme? That's my life! That's what I'm dealing with."

"Yes, but it's not all that you are dealing with. You and Carol aren't on drugs, but I bet that doesn't mean you're always happy together."

Lou thought back to the silent treatment Carol had given him on the flight the day before. She didn't like how he had handled Cory, and she communicated her displeasure by clamming up. Tears often lay just below the surface of her silence. Lou knew what her silence meant—that he, Lou, wasn't measuring up—and he resented it. He was having enough trouble with his boy; he didn't think he deserved the silent, teary lectures. "We're not perfect," Lou allowed.

"Nor am I with my wife, Lina," Yusuf said. "And you know what I've found? When Lina is upset with me in some way, the least helpful thing I can do is criticize her or try to correct her. When she's mad, she has her reasons. I might think she's wrong and her reasons illegitimate, but I've never once convinced her of that by fighting back." He looked at Lou and Carol. "How about you? Has it helped to try to change each other?"

Lou chewed tentatively on the inside of his cheek as he remembered rows he and Carol had gotten into over her silent treatment. "No, I suppose not," he finally answered. "Not generally, anyway."

"So for many problems in life," Yusuf said, "solutions will have to be deeper than strategies of discipline or correction."

Lou thought about that for a moment.

"But now for your harder question," Yusuf continued. "What if my child is doing something really harmful, like drugs? What then? Shouldn't I try to change him?"

"Exactly," Lou nodded.

"And the answer to that, of course," Yusuf said, "is yes."

This caught Lou by surprise, and he swallowed the retort he'd been planning.

"But I won't invite my child to change if my interactions with him are primarily in order to get him to change."

Lou got lost in that answer and furrowed his brow. He began to reload his objection.

"I become an agent of change," Yusuf continued, "only to the degree that I begin to live to help things go right rather than simply to correct things that are going wrong. Rather than simply correcting, for example, I need to reenergize my teaching, my helping, my listening, my learning. I need to put time and effort into building relationships. And so on. If I don't work the bottom part of the pyramid, I won't be successful at the top.

"Jenny, for example," he continued, "is currently outside on a wall refusing to join the others on the trail."

Still? Lou thought to himself.

"She doesn't want to enter the program," Yusuf continued. "That's understandable, really. What seventeen-year-old young woman is dying to spend sixty days sleeping on the hard ground and living on cornmeal and critters they can capture with homemade spears?"

"That's what they have to do out there?" Ria asked.

"Well, kind of," Yusuf smiled. "It's not quite that primitive."

"But it's close," Avi interjected with a chuckle.

Ria widened her eyes and rocked backward into her seat, trying to imagine how her boy would do in this environment. By contrast, her husband, Miguel, nodded approvingly.

"So what do we do?" Yusuf asked rhetorically. "Any attempt to discipline or to correct her behavior is unlikely to work, wouldn't you agree?"

"Oh, I don't know," Lou said, arguing more out of habit now than conviction. "If it were me, I would have gone over to her and told her to get her backside over to the vehicle."

"Right gentlemanly of you, Lou," Elizabeth quipped.

"And what if she had refused?" Yusuf asked.

Lou looked at Elizabeth. "Then I would have made her go," he said, carefully articulating each word.

"But Camp Moriah is a private organization with no authority of the state," Yusuf responded, "and no desire to create additional problems by trying to bully people into doing what we want them to do. We do not force children to enroll."

"Then you have a problem," Lou said.

"Yes, we certainly do," Yusuf agreed. "The same problem we each have in our families. And the same problem countries have with one another. We are all surrounded by other autonomous people who don't always behave as we'd like."

"So what can you do when that's the case?" Ria asked.

"Get really good at the deeper matters," Yusuf answered, "at helping things to go right."

"And how do you get good at that?" Ria followed up.

"That is exactly what we are here to talk about for the next two days," Yusuf answered. "Let's begin with the deepest matter of all, an issue I would like to introduce by going back some nine hundred years to a time when everything was going wrong."

3 · *Peace in Wartime*

"In June of 1099," Yusuf began, "Crusaders from the West laid siege to Jerusalem. After forty days, they penetrated the northern wall and flooded into the city. They slaughtered most of the city's Muslim population within two days. The last of the survivors were forced to carry the dead to mass unmarked graves, where they piled the corpses in heaps and set them on fire. These survivors were then either massacred or sold into slavery.

"The Jews, although not so numerous, fared no better. In the Jewish quarter, the inhabitants fled to the main synagogue for refuge. The invaders barricaded the exits and stacked wood around the building. They then torched it, burning all but the few who managed to escape. These people were slaughtered in the narrow streets as they attempted to flee.

"The brutality extended as well to the local Christians who officiated at Christian holy sites. These priests were expelled, tortured, and forced to disclose the location of precious relics, which were then taken from them.

"So began nearly two centuries of strife between invaders from the West and the people of the Middle East. In the minds of many in the Middle East, today's battles are a continuation of this ancient battle for the Holy Land. They view American and European powers as crusading invaders."

"As the lone European in the room," Elizabeth spoke up, "would you mind if I addressed the Crusades for a moment?"

"Not at all," Yusuf said. "Please."

"I know a little of this history. To begin with, it's important to understand the history of Jerusalem. It was Jewish through most of ancient times until Rome sacked it in 70 AD. Meanwhile, following the death of Christ, believers began to spread his gospel through the region. Christianity eventually became the official faith of the Roman Empire, and the faith quickly spread through all its territories, including Jerusalem. By 638 AD, the year Muslims captured Jerusalem, it had been a fully Christian city for three hundred years. So when the knights of the First Crusade took Jerusalem, in their minds they were retaking what had been taken from them. They, like the Muslims they were fighting, believed the city was rightfully theirs."

"That doesn't justify the atrocities, though," Pettis interjected.

"No," Elizabeth agreed, "it doesn't."

"Oh, but come on," Lou said, "the Crusaders didn't have a monopoly on atrocity. The Muslims' hands were dirty too."

"Were they?" Pettis asked. "I don't know the history. I'd be interested to hear."

"Lou is right about that," Elizabeth said. "There is ugliness on all sides of this conflict. Yusuf has already given us an example of atrocities by Westerners. An early Muslim example would be the massacre of the Banu Qurayza, the last Jewish tribe in Medina. In the earliest days of Islam, Muslim armies beheaded the entire tribe."

"And today they blow themselves up in order to maim and murder innocent civilians," Lou blurted.

Unhappy with the interruption, Elizabeth's mouth stretched disapprovingly into a line.

"I agree with Elizabeth that there are sordid details on all sides of this history," Yusuf said. "What I would like to introduce you to, however, is one not-so-sordid figure.

"After taking Jerusalem in 1099," he continued, "the Crusaders took control of most of the coastal areas of the Middle East. They continued to hold these regions for about eighty years. They succeeded largely because of infighting between rival Muslim military and political leaders. This began to change, however, with the rise to power of the Turkish sultan Nûr al-Dîn, who unified the various peoples of Syria. The tide turned entirely in favor of the Muslim resistance under his successor, Yûsuf Salâh al-Dîn, or simply 'Saladin,' as he is known in the West. Saladin united all the Muslim peoples from Syria to Egypt and mobilized their collective resistance. His armies recaptured Jerusalem in 1187.

"Militarily, politically, and in every other way, Saladin was the most successful leader of the period. His successes were so surprising and total that historians sometimes invoke luck and good fortune to explain them. However, as I have studied Saladin, I am convinced he succeeded in war for a much deeper reason; a reason that won't seem at first to be related to war at all."

"What?" Pettis asked. "What reason?"

"To understand it," Yusuf answered, "we need to get a better feel for the man. Let me tell you a story. On one occasion, an army scout came to Saladin with a sobbing woman from the enemy camp. She had requested, hysterically, that the scout take her to Saladin. She threw herself before Saladin, and said, 'Yesterday some Muslim thieves entered my tent and stole my little girl. I cried all through the night, believing I would never see her again. But our commanders told me that you, the king of the Muslims, are merciful.' She begged for his help.

"Saladin was moved to tears. He immediately sent one of his men to the slave market to look for the girl. They located her within the hour and returned her to her mother, whom they then escorted back to the enemy camp."

Yusuf paused for a moment. "If you were to research Saladin, you would discover that this story is characteristic. He was renowned for his kindness toward allies and enemies alike."

"I'm not sure those who died at the end of his army's swords thought him kind," Elizabeth interjected. "But I agree that in comparison to others of the period, he did shine a little brighter."

Lou was unimpressed. His mind drifted back to Vietnam and to all the dead young men his regiment had to carry out of the jungles. When he had returned from Vietnam, Lou made a personal point of visiting the mother of each soldier who had lost his life under his command. Over a period of two years, he visited fifty-three towns, from Seattle and San Diego in the West to Portland, Maine, in the East and Savannah, Georgia, in the South. He sat in the living rooms of the homes these men never returned to and held their grieving mothers in his arms as he told them of the heroic deeds of their sons. He loved his men. To this day, he still dreamed of ways he could have saved more of them. *Being kind and merciful is well and good,* he thought, *but they are traits that are poorly rewarded in wartime.*

"With that bit of background," Yusuf continued, "let me contrast Saladin's recapture of Jerusalem with the Crusaders' initial invasion. In the spring of 1187, after the Crusaders had broken a truce, Saladin called upon the forces of Islam to gather in Damascus. He planned to march against the occupiers in a unified effort and drive them from their lands."

"If I might," Elizabeth stepped in once more, "who was occupying whom was not entirely clear. As I mentioned before, each side viewed the other as an occupying force."

"Right," Yusuf said. "Sorry for the imprecision." Resuming, he said, "Saladin sprung a trap on the occupying—err, rather, Western—forces near the Sea of Galilee. A few escaped, including a leader named Balian of Ibelin. Balian escaped to Tyre, where via messenger he made a surprising request of Saladin: he asked whether he could go to Jerusalem and fetch his wife and bring her back to safety in Tyre. He promised he would not take up arms in defense of Jerusalem. Saladin agreed.

"However, upon arriving in Jerusalem and finding there was no one to lead its defense, Balian begged Saladin to let him out of his commitment. He wanted to stay and lead the resistance against Saladin's army. Saladin not only allowed it, he sent an escort to lead Balian's wife from Jerusalem to the safety of Tyre!"

Lou let out an audible harrumph.

"Yes, Lou, kind of hard to imagine, isn't it?"

"She must have been a looker, that's all I can say," Lou said, looking around for a laugh. Miguel obliged him, his eyes dancing with mirth as his broad shoulders rolled with laughter, but for the rest the joke fell flat. Carol shook her head ever so slightly and fought to remember that Lou was better on the inside than his outward bravado sometimes suggested. She knew that his behavior was being exacerbated by the stress he was feeling from having to be away from work when so much was going wrong there.

"The siege of Jerusalem began on the twentieth of September," Yusuf continued. "Nine days later, Saladin's men breached the wall close to the place where the Crusaders had flowed through almost ninety years earlier. Saladin put his men under strict order not to harm a single Christian person or plunder any of their possessions. He reinforced the guards at Christian places of worship and announced that the defeated peoples would be welcome to come to Jerusalem on pilgrimage whenever they liked.

"As a way to restock the treasury, Saladin worked out a ransom structure with Balian for each of the city's inhabitants. His men protested that the amounts were absurdly low. But Saladin was concerned for the poor among them. So much so, in fact, that he let many leave without any ransom whatsoever. He sent widows and children away with gifts. His leaders objected, saying that if they were going to let so many leave without any compensation, they should at least increase the ransom for the wealthy. But Saladin refused. Balian himself was allowed to leave with a rich sum. Saladin even sent an escort to protect him on his journey to Tyre."

Yusuf looked around at the group.

"He sounds disturbingly weak to me," Lou said.

"Yes," Yusuf said, "so weak that he was the most successful military leader of his era and remains revered to this day."

"He's still weak," Lou insisted. "And soft."

"Why do you say that, Lou?" Elizabeth interjected.

"Well," Lou began, "you heard what Yusuf said. He let all those people take advantage of him."

"You mean because he spared their lives?"

"And let them make off with the treasury."

"But they weren't in it for the treasury," she answered. "They were trying to establish a lasting victory."

"Then why not get rid of their enemies?" Lou objected. "Let them walk away and you just allow them to fight another day. Trust me, I fought in Vietnam. We would have been massacred there if that's what we had done."

Pettis spoke up. "We were massacred in Vietnam, Lou."

Lou's back went rigid. With eyes smoldering, he turned hard on Pettis. "Listen Pettis, why don't you stick to what you know, hmm? You have no idea what Vietnam was about—or about the heroism our men showed there."

"Air force," Pettis responded. "555th Tactical Fighter Squadron. Two tours." He looked calmly at Lou. "You?"

Lou was taken aback and muttered incomprehensibly under his breath before hurriedly saying, "Four years in 'Nam. Second Battalion, Ninth Marines—'Hell in a Helmet' as we called ourselves. Sorry," he added, nodding to Pettis.

Pettis nodded back. "No apology necessary."

"Two veterans in the group," Yusuf smiled enthusiastically. "Splendid!

"Lou," he continued, "you mentioned that Saladin sounds weak or soft."

Lou nodded, almost meekly this time.

"Do you suppose, however, that the defenders of the cities he captured one by one thought him weak? That rival Muslim leaders he subdued thought him weak? That those who had been defeated by no one else thought him weak?"

Lou hesitated momentarily. "No," he said in a more subdued tone. "I suppose not."

"No, they surely wouldn't have. And the reason why is simple: he *wasn't* weak. He was, in fact, remarkably and unfailingly strong. But he was something more than—or perhaps more accurately, deeper than—strong. And this extra something is what set him apart from all the others of his era who, although strong, were unsuccessful."

Yusuf paused.

"What was it?" Pettis asked. "This something extra, this something deeper."

"The most important factor in helping things go right."

"Which is?" Pettis followed up.

"The secret of Saladin's success in war," Yusuf answered, "was that his heart was at peace."

This was too much for Lou. "'Heart at peace' you say, Yusuf?" he asked with an edge to his voice. "That's your secret— that Saladin's heart was at peace?"

"Yes."

"You've got to be kidding," he said, looking first at Pettis and then at the others, with mocking eyes that culled for allies. He thought he found what he was looking for in Pettis, who seemed lost in thought, his brow deeply furrowed.

Lou then glanced at Elizabeth but couldn't read her countenance. He dug in once more, keeping her in his sight as he spoke. "So the secret to war is to have a heart at peace?" he asked mockingly, turning back to Yusuf.

"Yes, Lou," Yusuf answered unflinchingly. "And not just in war. It is the secret to success in business and family life as well. The state of your heart toward your children—whether at peace or at war—is by far the most important factor in this intervention we are now undertaking. It is also what will most determine your ability to successfully maneuver your company through the challenges created by your recent defections."

This comment knocked Lou completely off his stride. He was not accustomed to people standing up to his sarcasm, and Yusuf's even bolder development of his thesis and his pointed comment about Lou's corporate troubles caught Lou off guard.

He looked sideways at Carol, whom he surmised to have been the source of the inside information. She stared stiffly ahead, not acknowledging his gaze.

4 · *Beneath Behavior*

Just then, one of the young employees of the company walked in the room and whispered something to Yusuf. Excusing himself, Yusuf quickly followed the worker out of the room.

After he left, Pettis said to Avi, "I'm not sure what Yusuf meant by a heart being at peace. I'd like to hear more about that."

"Sure," Avi said. "To begin with, let's compare Saladin's recapture of Jerusalem to the earlier capture by the Crusaders." He looked at Pettis. "Do you notice any differences in the two victories?"

"Certainly," Pettis responded. "The Crusaders acted like barbarians."

"And Saladin?"

"He was almost humane. For someone who was attacking, anyway," he added.

"Say more about what you mean by humane," Avi invited.

Pettis paused to gather his thoughts. "What I mean," he finally said, "is that Saladin seems to have had regard for the people he was defeating. Whereas the crusading forces seem—well, they seem to have been barbaric, as I said before. They just massacred all those people as though they didn't matter at all."

"Exactly," Avi agreed. "To the initial crusading forces, the people *didn't* matter to them. That is, the Crusaders didn't really regard them as people so much as objects or chattel to be driven or exterminated at their will and pleasure.

"Saladin, on the other hand," Avi continued, "saw and honored the humanity of those he conquered. He may have wished they had never come to the borders of his lands, but he recognized these were people he was doing battle with, and that he therefore had to see, treat, and honor them as such."

"So what does that have to do with us?" Lou asked. "You're talking about a nine-hundred-year-old story, and a story about war at that. What does it have to do with our kids?" Thinking of what Yusuf had said about his company, he added, "And our employees?"

Avi looked squarely at Lou. "In every moment, we are choosing to be either like Saladin or like the crusading invaders. In the way we regard our children, our spouses, neighbors, colleagues, and strangers, we choose to see others either as people like ourselves or as objects. They either count like we do or they don't. In the former case, since we regard them as we regard ourselves, we say our hearts are at peace toward them. In the latter case, since we systematically view them as inferior, we say our hearts are at war."

"You seem to be pretty taken by Muslims' humanity toward others and others' inhumanity toward Muslims, Avi," Lou objected. "I'm afraid that is quite naive." He thought of what he knew of Avi's history. "And surprising, coming from one whose own father was killed by the people you are lauding."

Avi heaved a heavy sigh. "Yusuf and I have been speaking of no one, Lou, but Saladin. There are those who see humanely and those who don't in every country and faith community. Lumping everyone of a particular race or culture or faith into a single stereotype is a way of failing to see them as people. We are trying, here, to avoid that mistake, and it seems to me that Saladin is a person we could learn from."

Lou fell silent in the face of this rebuke. He was beginning to feel lonely among the group.

"The contrast between Saladin's taking of Jerusalem and the Crusaders' taking of Jerusalem," Avi continued, "teaches an important lesson: almost any behavior—even behavior as stark as war—can be done in two different ways." At this, he went to the board and drew the following:

THE WAY-OF-BEING DIAGRAM

BEHAVIORS
Invading Jerusalem
Paying people from treasury

WAY OF BEING

Heart at Peace
Others are PEOPLE:
Hopes, needs, cares,
and fears as real to
me as my own

Heart at War
Others are OBJECTS:
Obstacles
Vehicles
Irrelevancies

"Think about it," Avi said, turning to face the group. "The Saladin story suggests that there is something deeper than our behavior—something philosophers call our 'way of being,' or our regard for others. The philosopher Martin Buber demonstrated that at all times, no matter what we might be doing, we are always in the world in either an 'I-It' or 'I-Thou' way. In other words, we are always seeing others either as objects—as obstacles, for example, or as vehicles or irrelevancies—or we are seeing them as people. To put it in terms of the Saladin story, there are two ways to take Jerusalem: from people or from objects."

"Who cares how you take it, then," Lou blurted, suddenly feeling energized for another round. "If you have to take it you have to take it. It's just that simple. A soldier doesn't have the luxury of worrying about the life of the person who is staring down his lance or barrel. In fact, it would be dangerous to invite him to consider that life. He might hesitate when he needs to fire."

This comment crystallized a doubt that had been creeping up within Pettis as well. "Yes, Lou, that's a good point," he said. "What about that?" he asked Avi. "Lou's worry about soldiers seeing their enemies as people is legitimate, is it not? I see problems with that as well."

"It seems like it might be a problem, doesn't it?" Avi agreed. "But was it a problem for Saladin?"

"Yes, it was," Lou retorted, emboldened by Pettis's support. "He was completely taken advantage of by the enemies he let leave with Jerusalem's riches."

"Do you suppose seeing others as people means that we have to let them leave with riches? That it means we must let others take advantage of us?" Avi responded.

"Well, it seems like it does, yes," Lou answered. "At least, that's what it seems you've been implying."

"No, that's not his point," Elizabeth disagreed. "Look at the diagram, Lou. You have the behaviors at the top and the two basic ways of seeing others at the bottom. Avi's saying that everything he's written in the behavior area—taking Jerusalem, for example, or paying people from the treasury—can be done in either of those ways of being, with a heart at peace or a heart at war."

"Well then who cares which way you do it?" Lou repeated. "If you need to take Jerusalem, just take Jerusalem. Who cares which way you do it? Just get on with it!"

Avi looked thoughtfully at Lou. "Cory cares," he said.

"Huh?"

"Cory cares."

"He cares about *what*?"

"He cares whether he's being seen as a person or an object."

Lou didn't say anything.

"Seeing an equal person as an inferior object is an act of violence, Lou. It hurts as much as a punch to the face. In fact, in many ways it hurts more. Bruises heal more quickly than emotional scars do."

Lou looked as if he were about to respond to this but finally didn't, slouching back in his chair as he argued with himself about his son.

"The inhabitants of Jerusalem surely cared as well," Avi continued. "But even more than that, *you* care, Lou," he added. "You care whether you are being seen as a person or as an object. In fact, there is little you care more about than this."

"Then you don't know anything about me," Lou retorted, shaking his head in disagreement. "I couldn't care less what others think about me. Just ask my wife."

The sad irony of his comment, as autobiographical as it was on this particular day, didn't penetrate Lou. At his side, Carol blushed slightly, clearly unready for the attention that suddenly came her way.

Avi smiled good-naturedly. "Actually, Lou, I think you do care."

"Then you think wrong."

"Maybe," Avi allowed, nodding. "It wouldn't be the first

time. But here's something to consider: has it been important to you to get others to agree with you this morning?"

Lou remembered his earlier hope that Elizabeth shared his views and the energy he felt when it appeared that Pettis did.

"If so, you do care," Avi continued. "But ultimately, you are the only one who will be able to answer that question."

Lou felt a tingle of pain, the way one does when a foot or limb has been asleep and is just beginning to revive itself.

"This issue of way of being is of great practical importance," Avi continued. "First of all, think of a difficult business situation—say a complicated negotiation, for example. Who do you think would be more likely to put together a deal in difficult circumstances, a negotiator who sees the others in the negotiation as objects or one who sees them as people?"

This question piqued Lou's interest, as he was in the middle of a union negotiation that was going nowhere.

"The one who sees others as people," Pettis responded. "Definitely."

"Why?" Avi asked.

"Because whether you're talking about negotiators or anyone else, people don't like dealing with jerks. They'd just as soon poke jerks in the eye as help them."

Avi chuckled. "That's true, isn't it," he agreed. "In fact, have you noticed that we sometimes choose to poke another in the eye even when doing so harms our own position?"

This question swept Lou's thoughts back to an emergency meeting just two weeks earlier. Kate Stenarude, Jack Taylor, Nelson Mumford, Kirk Weir, and Don Shilling—five of Lou's six key executives—were standing in their places at the Zagrum Company's boardroom table, giving Lou an earful. They were leaving, they told him, unless Lou gave them more space to run their organizations. They called him a meddler, a micro-manager, and a control freak. One of them (Jack Taylor, Lou vowed never to forget) even painted Lou a tyrant.

Lou had listened to all of it in silence, not even looking into their faces. But he was burning inside. *Ingrates!* he had growled to himself. *Incompetent, bumbling, turncoat ingrates!*

"Get the hell out then!" he had finally yelled. "If the standards here are too high for you, then you'd better leave now because they're not coming down!"

"We're not talking about the standards, Lou," Kate had pleaded. "We're talking about the atmosphere of oppression we've come to work under. The ladder thing you just pulled on me, for example." She was referring to how Lou had recently removed a ladder from the sales team area, an act that symbolically undercut her attempt to implement a new incentive system in her department. "It's a small thing, but it speaks volumes."

"It's only oppressive for those who can't measure up to the standards, Kate," he spat back, ignoring her specific complaint. "And honestly, Kate, after all I've done for you." He shook his head in disgust. "You owe everything you've become here to me, and now look at you." He curled up his lip as if he would spit the whole lot of them out of his mouth if he could. "I would have expected more out of you.

"So get out then! All of you. Get the hell out!"

The March Meltdown, as this interchange and subsequent defection had come to be called around the halls of Zagrum Company, had nearly ground Zagrum's work to a halt over the last two weeks. Lou was worried about his company's future.

"Viewed economically," Avi continued, pulling Lou back to the present, "this is an insane strategy. But we do it anyway. In fact, it's almost like we feel compelled to do it. We can get ourselves in a position where we compulsively act in ways that

make our own lives more difficult—by stoking the fires of resentment in a spouse, for example, or anger in a child. But we
do it anyway. Which leads us to the first reason why way of being
is so important: when our hearts are at war, we can't see clearly.
We give ourselves the best opportunity to make clear-minded
decisions only to the extent that our hearts are at peace."

Lou thought about that as he pondered his decisions regarding Kate and the others who had left him.

"Here's another reason why way of being is so important,"
Avi continued. "Think about the negotiation situation again.
The most successful negotiators understand the other side's
concerns and worries as much as their own. But who is more
likely to be able to consider and understand the other side's
positions so fully—the person who sees others as objects or the
person who sees them as people?"

"The one who sees people," Ria answered. Pettis and most
of the others nodded in agreement.

"I think that's right," Avi said. "People whose hearts are at
war toward others can't consider others' objections and challenges enough to be able to find a way through them."

Lou thought of the impasse with the union.

"Finally," Avi said, "let me add a third reason why way of
being is important. Think about your experiences over the last
few years with the children you have brought to us. Have you
ever felt like they reacted unfairly to you even when you were
bending over backwards to be kind and fair to them?"

Lou's mind drifted back to an exchange he and Cory had
had just two mornings earlier. "So it's all my fault, right Dad?"
Cory had bellowed sarcastically. "You're the great Lou Herbert
who has never made a mistake in his life, right?"

"Don't be a child," Lou remembered responding, proud
that he was able to remain so calm in the face of such disrespect.

"It must be pretty embarrassing having a son like me—an addict, a thief. Right?"

Lou didn't say anything, and he congratulated himself for rising above the moment. As he thought about it, however, he had to admit Cory was right. Lou was distinctly proud of his two older children—Mary, twenty-four, a PhD candidate at MIT; and Jesse, twenty-two, a senior at Lou's alma mater, Syracuse University. In comparison, he found Cory embarrassing. That was true.

"Well, let me tell you something, Daaaad," Cory had continued, sarcastically drawing out the word for emphasis. "Being the son of Lou Herbert is a living hell, to tell you the truth. Do you know what it feels like knowing that your dad thinks you're a loser?

"Yeah, I know you're thinking, 'but you are a loser.' I've been hearing that from you for years. I was never as good as Mary or Jesse. At least, not to you. Well, let me tell you something. You're not as good as Mom, or any other adult I know, for that matter. You're a bigger loser as a parent than I'll ever be as a son. And you're just as much of a disaster at work. Why else would Kate and the others have walked out on you!"

This exchange had once again showed Lou that treating Cory civilly got him nowhere. Cory disrespected him whether Lou yelled or stayed silent.

"I'm going to suggest something to you about this," Avi continued, pulling Lou and the others back from their thoughts. "It's an idea you might want to resist at first, especially regarding your children. But here it is: Generally speaking, we respond to others' way of being toward us rather than to their behavior. Which is to say that our children respond more to how we're regarding them than they do to our particular words or actions.

We can treat our children fairly, for example, but if our hearts are warring toward them while we're doing it, they won't think they're being treated fairly at all. In fact, they'll respond to us as if they weren't being treated fairly."

Avi looked at the group. "As important as behavior is," he said, "most problems at home, at work, and in the world are not failures of strategy but failures of way of being. As we've discussed, when our hearts are at war, we can't see situations clearly, we can't consider others' positions seriously enough to solve difficult problems, and we end up provoking hurtful behavior in others.

"If we have deep problems, it's because we are failing at the deepest part of the solution. And when we fail at this deepest level, we invite our own failure."

5 · *The Pattern of Conflict*

"Actually," Avi said, "when our hearts are at war, we not only *invite* failure, we *invest* in it. Let me give you an example.

"One Saturday," he began, "I returned home at about 5:45 p.m., just fifteen minutes before I was to meet a friend for tennis. Problem was, I had also promised my wife, Hannah, that I would mow the lawn."

There were a few knowing chuckles around the room.

"Well, I raced to the garage, pulled out the lawn mower, and mowed it in a sprint. I then ran back into the house to get dressed for tennis. As I raced past Hannah toward the stairs, I mumbled that I was going to meet my friend Paul for a game of tennis. I was just about to the stairs when Hannah called after me, 'Are you going to edge?'

"I stopped in my tracks. 'It doesn't need edging,' I said. 'Not this time.'

"'I think it does,' she said.

"'Oh come on,' I objected. 'No one is going to pass our house and say, "Look, Marge, the Rozens didn't edge!" It isn't going to happen!' This didn't sway her in the least, so I added, 'Besides, I ran the wheels of the mower up on the cement as I cut around the edges. It looks fine.'

"'You said you were going to mow,' she said, 'and that means edging too.'

"'No it doesn't!' I countered. 'Mowing means mowing; edging means edging. You don't have to edge every time you mow.

That's ridiculous. Besides, I'm already late for tennis. Do you want Paul just to be waiting? Is that what you want?'

"I thought I had her at that, but then she said, 'Okay, I guess I'll edge then.'"

The knowing chuckles returned. "Guilt-tripping you, wasn't she?" Miguel spoke up for the first time that morning, in a gravelly voice that matched his appearance. His wife, Ria, didn't look too pleased by the comment.

"Exactly," Avi said. "I didn't want her doing it, so I told her that maybe I could edge when I got back. And with that, I threw on my tennis gear and left.

"I didn't get home until after dark. I'd beaten Paul for the first time and was feeling pretty happy. I went into the kitchen, opened the fridge, and poured myself a large glass of orange juice. Hannah walked into the room when I was in the middle of a long guzzle. I quickly dropped the glass from my mouth and was about to say, 'I beat Paul!' when she asked, 'Are you going to edge?'

"The excitement drained from me in an instant, and I was immediately back in the irritated emotional place I had been a couple of hours earlier.

"'You've been sitting around here wondering for the last two hours whether I'm going to edge?' I badgered. 'That's *pathetic*.'

"'But you said you would when you got back,' she replied.

"I shot back at her: 'I said *maybe* I would. But that was before I knew it was going to be pitch black.'

"'But you said you'd do it.'

"'Do you want me to put out my eye or something?' I retorted. 'Is that what you want? It's pitch black. I wouldn't be able to wear my sunglasses.'

"'Then I'll edge,' she said."

"Hell, let her do it!" Lou bellowed. "If she wants it done that badly, she should just do it herself."

A few people chuckled at that, Miguel especially. Carol pursed her lips.

"Well, I didn't do that, Lou," Avi responded. "Instead, I raised my head piously high, inhaled deeply, and said, 'Okay. I'll edge to keep peace in the family.' And then I stalked to the garage, pulled out the Weed Eater, and edged for two solid hours. If she wanted edging, she was going to get edging!"

A few in the group laughed at that as well. Miguel chortled so hard he nearly choked.

"But think about it," Avi continued. "When I came back in the house, do you think my edging had kept peace in the family?"

The participants all shook their heads—even Lou, although he was barely aware of it.

"And it didn't keep peace in the family for one simple reason: my heart was still at war toward Hannah. She seemed just as small-minded, inconsiderate, demanding, unreasonable, and cold when I was edging as when I wasn't. The change in my outward behavior didn't change how I was feeling about her. In fact, if anything, the more I edged in the darkness, the worse she seemed to me. When I chewed up a piece of the fence because I couldn't see well, I felt a perverse sense of satisfaction. It proved how unreasonable Hannah was being.

"As you might imagine, when I finally came back in the house, our feelings toward each other poked through every word, look, and gesture. In fact, if anything, we were less civil to each other than before—which ticked me off all the more, by the way. Here I had put my own eyesight at risk by doing what she unreasonably demanded, and she was still mad at me! *The least she could do is be grateful*, I told myself. *But no, she's impossible to please!*"

Miguel started coughing in laughter. He brought his barrel-shaped fist to his mouth to try to quell the eruption.

"What is it, Miguel?" Avi asked.

He raised his hand in front of him, telling Avi to wait a moment while he got himself under control.

Avi broke out into a big grin himself, as he watched this large man struggle to choke off a case of the laughs.

Clearing his throat, Miguel finally said in a pinched voice, "Sorry. Your story reminded me o' somethin'," he said. "Happened two nights ago."

Ria's eyes widened as she turned to look at him.

"I had to do the dishes. Knew Ria would have a cow if I didn't. Even though I had to work early in the mornin'."

Lou smiled to himself at the image of this hulk of a man leaning over the sink, dutifully washing the dishes.

"And then," Miguel continued, "when I finished, she came in. Started snoopin'. Wanted to see if I'd done it."

"I did not!" Ria objected, too strongly.

"Yes you did. Like always."

"I was just coming in to get something to eat."

"Right," he laughed. "That's why you were lookin' in the sink? For food?"

Now it was Lou who burst out laughing.

Ria's face started to turn pink. "Well, I wouldn't have to do that if you would just clean up like you should," she shot back.

Miguel shook his head.

"I take it you mentioned this, Miguel," Avi interrupted, "because you felt these warring feelings we're talking about?"

"That's right. But who wouldn't? Right? She just said it herself," he said pointing at Ria. "She's always hoverin'. Checks what I do. Doesn't think it's good enough."

Carol stirred beside Lou. "Maybe she's not hovering, Miguel. Maybe she's just tired of having to do everything."

Lou was aghast, partly because he was feeling a kinship with Miguel at the moment and partly because it was so unlike Carol to put someone on the spot. "What did Miguel do to you, Carol?" he said. "Maybe this woman should be grateful her man will do the dishes even though he carries the burden of making a living."

"Oh, so women don't have their share of burdens, Lou?" It was the woman Lou had noticed at the back of the room before they started but had not met. She had tired of Lou's domination of the dialogue and could restrain herself no longer. "Including career burdens?" she continued. "Are you saying that only men know about that? For that matter, perhaps women don't even have names in your mind. Maybe we're all just this woman or that woman. Even worse, maybe I'm just that *black* woman. Is that the way it is? Should we all just be happy for what we're able to do for you? Is that the way it is in your house, and in your company?"

Lou felt blindsided. He was about to pounce when Avi interrupted. "Hearts at war, that's what we're talking about," he said. "Gwyn, Lou, Carol, Miguel, Ria, the rest of us—do you feel what I mean? How are we seeing each other—right now? As allies? As enemies? These are warring feelings."

Lou glanced over at his assailant, who was seated on the other side of Elizabeth. *So her name is Gwyn,* he noted.

Avi paused for a moment. "Go ahead, look around," he said. "Are we seeing people, or are we seeing objects?"

Most in the room avoided each other's eyes despite the invitation to look.

"When we start seeing others as objects," Avi continued, "we begin provoking them to make our lives difficult. We actually start inviting others to make us miserable. We begin provoking in others the very things we say we hate."

"How so?" Lou asked.

"Can't you feel it?" Avi asked. "How our emotions are beginning to run away from us, and how we are beginning to provoke hostile comments and feelings in each other?"

Lou had to admit he could feel it.

"We see the same pattern in my story with Hannah," he continued. "Let's diagram it, and I think you'll see what I mean.

"To begin with," he said, "Hannah asked me to edge, didn't she? And then complained and badgered me when I objected." He then drew the following on the board:

THE COLLUSION DIAGRAM

AVI	HANNAH
3. I DO	**4. SHE SEES**
2. I SEE	**1. SHE DOES** Insists I do as she asks Complains Badgers

←

"Why are you calling this collusion?" Pettis asked.

"For reasons that will become clearer in a few minutes," Avi answered. "Make sure I come back to that, will you?"

Pettis nodded.

"When Hannah asked me to edge," Avi continued, "how do you suppose I began to see or regard her?"

"As demanding," Miguel answered. Glancing at Ria, he added, "Unreasonable too."

Avi wrote this in the area he had marked with a 2.

"Let's face it," Lou said, "she was a nag, plain and simple. Not saying she always is; Hannah's probably a wonderful lady. But in this case, she should have just done it herself and stopped complaining."

"Okay, Lou," Avi chuckled, as he added "nag" to the board. "Would it be fair to say I was seeing her as an object?"

"As an obstacle, definitely," Lou answered.

Avi added this as well.

"So when I was seeing Hannah—as we've listed here at number 2—as a nag and so on, how did I act? What did I do?"

THE COLLUSION DIAGRAM

AVI	HANNAH
3. I DO	**4. SHE SEES**
↑	
2. I SEE	**1. SHE DOES**
An Object:	Insists I do
Demanding	as she asks
Unreasonable	Complains
Nag	Badgers

←

"You protested," Gwyn answered. "You didn't think you should have to do it, and you told her so. A bit childishly too I might add."

Avi smiled good-naturedly. "Yes, thank you, Gwyn."

"Oh, you're most welcome," she said, the edge still in her voice.

"So I protested," Avi repeated, while adding that in the area he had marked as number 3. "What else did I do?"

"I would say you were trying to help her see the situation more reasonably," Elizabeth said. "I don't think you were being childish necessarily," she added. "Bothered, certainly, but not childish. After all, you mowed even though you didn't have the time. You were just trying to make your appointment."

"Yes, *his* appointment," Gwyn said. "That's just the point. Maybe she had plans of her own. What about what she wanted to do? Shouldn't that matter?"

"Okay, Gwyn, tell me," Lou interjected. "What plans of Hannah's required that Avi edge the lawn, and right then? What would that have to do with *her* plans, assuming she had any?"

"'Assuming she had any?'" Gwyn repeated mockingly. "Can't women have plans, Lou?"

"Of course they can have plans. That's not what I'm saying. But don't make me your plan. Don't try to run my life and then act like I'm violating your civil rights if I don't do just what you want me to do."

"So you're a racist as well," Gwyn shot back with an I-figured-as-much nod.

"'Racist'? What are you talking about? What's your problem, lady? What did I ever do to you?"

"Gwyn, Lou," Avi said in an imploring tone, "let's hold on here. We might disagree about a lot of things, but how we do it makes a big difference. If we start seeing each other as objects, we'll get to the point where we'll need to see each other as disagreeable rather than as simply disagreeing. Once that happens, we'll end up provoking each other just as Hannah and I did. Let's not fall into the very trap we're seeking to understand and avoid."

This comment, like Avi's invitation a couple of minutes earlier, appeared to lessen some of the rancor in the room. But Avi knew this was mostly illusion. Anger—or more precisely, war—was brewing just beneath the surface and threatening to sweep away their thoughts and emotions.

"Let's come back to the story," he said.

THE COLLUSION DIAGRAM

AVI	HANNAH

3. I DO	4. SHE SEES
Protest	
Teach her	
Comply with	
attitude	

$\rightarrow$

$\uparrow$

2. I SEE	1. SHE DOES
An Object:	Insists I do
Demanding	as she asks
Unreasonable	Complains
Nag	Badgers

$\leftarrow$

"So I protested to Hannah," he said, pointing at the area marked 3, "and tried to teach her. And then, of course, I even ended up edging. In fact, I edged with a kind of ferocious intensity, didn't I—with an attitude?"

Most in the room nodded.

"Given how I acted and how I was seeing Hannah, how do you suppose she saw me?"

"As self-centered," Gwyn answered.

"And inconsiderate," said Ria.

"And immature," added Gwyn.

"Yes, okay. Thanks. I think," Avi smiled wryly, adding these comments to area 4. "So let's look at this situation," he said, backing away from the board.

THE COLLUSION DIAGRAM

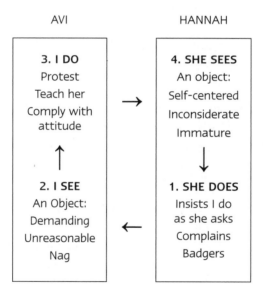

"If Hannah is seeing me as we've listed here at number 4— as self-centered, inconsiderate, and immature—is she now less or more likely to insist that I do as she says and to complain when I don't?"

"More," the group answered.

"So she'll do more of what we've listed here at number 1, which means that I'll see and do more of what we've listed at numbers 2 and 3, and she'll then see and do more of what we've listed at numbers 4 and 1! Around and around we'll go, each of us provoking in the other the very things we're complaining about." He paused to let that settle. "Think about it," he said. "Each of us ends up inviting the very behaviors we say we hate in the other!"

"But that's crazy," Pettis observed.

"Yes, Pettis, it is. And because it is, we call this *collusion* rather than merely *conflict*."

Pettis puzzled on that. "I'm not sure I understand the distinction."

"The word 'conflict' is passive," Avi responded. "It is something that happens *to* us. For example, something we refer to as a conflict might simply be the result of a misunderstanding. But many conflicts aren't that way at all. Many conflicts are like the one we've been considering: they involve situations where the parties are actively engaged in perpetuating the trouble. In such cases, far from being passive victims of misunderstanding, we become active perpetuators of misunderstanding. The word 'collusion' captures this element of active participation more accurately than 'conflict' does, so we use it to describe conflicts where the parties are actually inviting the very things they're fighting against." At this, Avi wrote the following on the board:

COLLUSION:
A conflict where the parties are inviting the very things they're fighting against

"And you're right," Avi continued, "this is insane. And yet this insanity prevails in large areas of our lives. It describes much of what happens between spouses who are struggling, parents and children who are battling, coworkers who are competing, and countries that are fighting." Avi looked around at the group. "It also describes what has just been happening in this room, doesn't it? We're beginning to provoke in others the very comments and behaviors we are accusing them of.

"Despite the insanity of it, this pattern of interpersonal and inner violence can come to rule our lives and the lives of the organizations and countries where we work and live.

"In fact," he continued, "this insanity tries to spread.

"Let me show you how."

6 · *Escalation*

"Look around the room," Avi invited once more. "Who would you want to gather with and talk to if we were to take a break? Go ahead," he invited. "Look around."

Gwyn glanced furtively at Ria and Carol. Miguel looked quickly at Lou, but then turned away when Lou turned to him. Lou looked inquiringly at Elizabeth, but she didn't acknowledge him. She seemed not to want to be included in this pairing off.

"And what would you be likely to talk about with these people?" Avi asked.

There was a silence in the room, but eyes darted here and there, and it was clear to Avi that the group was responding silently to his question.

"Gwyn," Avi said, interrupting the silence, "if I might be so bold as to ask, Who in the room would you most like to talk to, and what do you think your conversations might be about?"

"Oh, probably Ria, I'd say. And maybe Carol. And what would we talk about? About their husbands I'd imagine," she answered, with a wry smile.

"And what about their husbands?" Avi asked.

"Whether they're always so bigoted or only when they're in public."

Avi butted in before Lou could fire back.

"Notice what's happened here," Avi said. "Gwyn ends up talking with Ria and Carol. And about what? About how they are each being treated unfairly or unjustly by someone else. We end up gathering with allies—actual, perceived, or potential—as a way of feeling justified in our own accusing views of others.

"As a result of this fact, conflicts try to spread."

Adding more boxes to the diagram on the board, he said, "Like this."

THE COLLUSION DIAGRAM

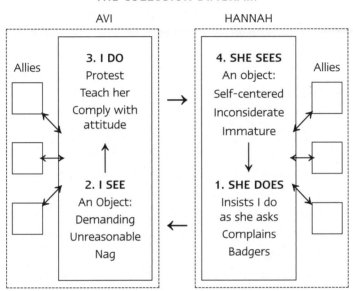

"So what begins as a conflict between two people spreads to a conflict between many as each person enlists others to his or her side. Everyone begins acting in ways that invite more of the very problem from the other side that each is complaining about! We have seen it happen here in this room in the last few minutes. It certainly happened that way in my home as Hannah and I found ways to recruit our children into the fray. I would conspicuously roll my eyes, for example, when Hannah demanded something of me. And I would commiserate with the children when I thought she was coming down too hard on them. I recruited my kids into feeling mistreated like I felt."

"That's sick," Gwyn said.

"Yes," Avi agreed, "it is.

"And I would wager a mighty sum," he continued, "that your respective organizations look like this as well—with workers recruiting colleagues and others with the tales they tell, leading to organizations that are divided into warring silos, one group complaining incessantly about another, and the other returning the same. Until finally, your organizations are filled with people whose energies are largely spent on sustaining conflict—what we call collusion—and who therefore are not fully focused on achieving the productive goals of the organization.

"Am I right?" Avi asked with emphasis.

Although he didn't say anything, Lou had to admit that he saw this pattern in spades at Zagrum. He could also see himself and Cory spinning in the same kind of circle. The harder he was on Cory, the more Cory rebelled, and the more Cory rebelled, the more Lou bore down on him. Lou didn't roll his eyes like Avi did, but he gathered allies by complaining about Cory to Carol and others.

"It seems to me like many world-level conflicts are collusions as well," Elizabeth spoke up. "The conflict in my region of the world in Northern Ireland, for example. Both sides are inviting the very things they're fighting against."

"It's the same way in the conflict between Israelis and Palestinians," Avi agreed. "In fact," he continued, "the concept of collusion explains how an ancient personal conflict now threatens the entire world. Consider the story of Abraham and his sons, Isaac and Ishmael. These sons, in accordance with decrees attributed in scripture to God, became fathers of nations—Isaac the father of the Israelite people and Ishmael the father of the Arab people. As such, these men hold special places in the belief systems of Jews, Christians, and Muslims the world over.

"Jews and Christians, for their part, believe that Isaac was the chosen son with specific rights granted to him and his posterity, including rights to the land. They believe that God told Abraham to offer Isaac as a sacrifice as a test of Abraham's faith. According to the Old Testament, this sacrifice was to take place on a hill 'in the land of Moriah'—a location in present-day Jerusalem. Centuries later, King Solomon constructed a temple on a hill in Jerusalem believed to be the location of this event, a mount known as Mount Moriah—the mountain after which Camp Moriah is named. In modern times, this mount is capped by the Al Aqsa Mosque complex, originally constructed by the Muslims after the initial conquest of Jerusalem that Elizabeth told us about. The world-famous shrine known as the Dome of the Rock, located within the thirty-five-acre complex, occupies the spot from where Muslims believe the prophet Mohammed ascended to heaven in a nocturnal vision. It is also believed to be the place of the experience between Abraham and his son.

"Which brings us to Ishmael.

"Although the Koran does not tell us one way or the other, many Muslims believe it was Ishmael, not Isaac, that Abraham was commanded to sacrifice on Moriah. Muslims also believe that Ishmael, rather than Isaac, was the chosen son. And finally, they believe it was Ishmael, not Isaac, who was given the right to the land. And so we have a dispute between brothers—those who believe Isaac was the chosen son and those who look to Ishmael as the chosen one. Descendants of each believe that they have claim to the land and to the heritage and primary blessings of the prophet Abraham."

Avi pointed at the collusion diagram. "You could substitute Isaac for my name and Ishmael for Hannah's and the diagram would be equally true of that conflict. Believers on each side now provoke the very mistreatment from the other that they are complaining about."

"But what if one of the views is the correct one, Avi?" Lou interjected. "Are you suggesting that all parties in a conflict are equally in the wrong, even if one side's claims are patently false?"

"And which side's claims are patently false here, Lou?" The heads of the group whipped around. It was Yusuf, who had slipped back into the room unnoticed a minute or two before.

"Well, Yusuf," Lou answered, after resizing him up for a moment, "I would say that yours are."

"Mine?"

"Yes."

"And which claims would mine be?"

Lou instantly regretted the presumptuousness that left him open to such an easy counter. "Well, I guess I don't know what your individual views are, exactly, Yusuf," he said, trying to cover the crack left exposed by his earlier answer. "I was speaking rather of your people's views."

"Oh? And what people would that be?"

"Ishmael's descendants," Lou answered with a forced non-chalance. "The Arab people."

Yusuf nodded. "Another characteristic of conflicts such as these," he said, gesturing toward the board, "is the propensity to demonize others. One way we do this is by lumping others into lifeless categories—bigoted whites, for example, lazy blacks, crass Americans, arrogant Europeans, violent Arabs, manipulative Jews, and so on. When we do this, we make masses of unknown people into objects and many of them into our enemies."

"I'm not making anyone into my enemy, Yusuf. I'm merely naming those who have declared me to be their enemy."

"And all Arabs have done this?" Yusuf asked. "And they have named you, Lou Herbert, as their enemy?"

At first, Lou was beaten back by this question, but then he leaned back in his chair, a sudden air of rediscovered confidence dancing in his eyes. "Why do you insist on changing the subject?"

"I don't think I have, Lou."

"Oh yes you have," Lou countered. "You keep answering my questions with unrelated questions. You don't want to go where my questions are directed, so you create mirages elsewhere."

Yusuf didn't say anything.

"I'll tell you what, Yusuf. I'll answer your questions after you answer mine."

"Fair enough," Yusuf said. "What would you like me to answer?"

7 · *The Right Thing and the Right Way*

"Okay, first of all," Lou began, "I asked whether it makes a difference in a conflict if one side is in the right and the other in the wrong. So I ask you again: doesn't that matter?"

"Yes," Yusuf replied, "it does matter. But not the way you think it does."

"What is that supposed to mean?"

"Well, Lou," Yusuf responded measuredly, "have you ever been in a conflict with someone who thought he was wrong?"

Lou thought of Cory and the boardroom meeting with his five mutinous executives.

"No," he answered coolly. "But that doesn't mean they're not."

"True," Yusuf agreed. "But you see, no conflict can be solved so long as all parties are convinced they are right. Solution is possible only when at least one party begins to consider how he might be wrong."

"But what if I'm not wrong!" Lou blurted.

"If you are not wrong, then you will be willing to consider how you might be mistaken."

"What kind of twisted riddle is that?"

Yusuf smiled. "It only seems like a riddle, Lou, because we are so unaccustomed to considering the impact of what is below our words, our actions, and our thoughts. There are two ways to seize Jerusalem or to engage in almost any other strategy or behavior, as Avi discussed with you. Which means there is a way I can be wrong even if taking Jerusalem is the best—even the right—thing to do. If I don't remain open to how I might be mistaken in this deeper way, I might live out my life convinced I was on the right side of a given conflict, but I won't have found lasting solutions.

"The deepest way in which we are right or wrong," he continued, "is in our *way of being* toward others. I can be right on the surface—in my behavior or positions—while being entirely mistaken beneath, in my way of being. I might, for example, yell at my kids about the importance of chores and be entirely correct about their importance. However, do you suppose I invite the help and cooperation I am wanting from them when my heart is at war in my yelling?"

Lou's mind reverted to Cory and to how he had found it difficult to speak a civil word to him for nearly two years.

"So, Lou," Yusuf continued, "in your conflicts with others, even if you are convinced you have been right in the positions you've taken, can you say with confidence that you have also been right in your *way of being* toward them? Can you say that you have been seeing them as people rather than as objects in your disagreements, and that your heart has therefore been at peace rather than at war toward them?"

Lou, still silent, slumped slightly in his chair. He knew that the answer to this question was obvious to everyone in the room. Not only was his heart not at peace toward others, it seemed too often to revel in interpersonal warfare.

This thought transported him back in memory once more.

Lou had grown up in Athens, New York, a picturesque town located on the Hudson River 120 miles north of Manhattan and 30 miles south of Albany. His father was an apple farmer who worked around the clock seven days a week to eke out a meager living. They lived in a Civil War–era white clapboard farmhouse that sat only fifty yards off the west bank of the Hudson.

Their farm was a rather modest ten acres, but it was the prettiest parcel in Greene County, occupying a peninsula that jutted out into the Hudson. From the top floor of the farmhouse, one could see the Catskill Mountains rising above the trees to the west. The setting was so beautiful that Lou's father could never bring himself to leave, even though he could have run a far grander operation elsewhere.

Through Lou's youth, the family had owned only one vehicle—a red 1942 farm truck with a matching red four-foot-tall wooden bay on the flatbed. The truck rattled and coughed like a ninety-year-old chain-smoker. Lou grew up thinking that the shoulder of the road was merely a second lane, as his father nearly always hugged the grasses that lined the streets in order to let other vehicles pass.

It was no small thing, then, when the Herberts purchased a new car. Lou was sixteen at the time, and he was eager to show the car to his friends in town. The day after his father brought it home, Lou asked if he could take it for some errands. Sensing his son's excitement, Lou's father readily agreed.

Lou ran out to the driveway and started it up. The low hum of the engine exhilarated him and he stroked the dash in anticipation. Just then he remembered he had left his wallet in the house and ran in to get it. When he raced back out, to his horror, the car had vanished! Lou remembered his feeling of panic, and then the awful thought that the car might have rolled down the slope of the approach and spilled off the driveway and into the Hudson.

Didn't I put it back in park? Lou had screamed in his mind as he ran down the drive. *Didn't I set the brake?*

Where the lane turned, sure enough, fresh tire tracks headed down the hill toward the river. Lou sprinted to the edge of the bluff and looked some twenty feet down. There looking back at him were the headlights of his father's car. He stood frozen as the water slowly sucked the car under the surface and out of sight.

Lou remembered walking numbly up to the house, wondering how he could break the news to his father. He entered the farmhouse and saw his father facing away from him in his favorite wingback chair. He was reading the newspaper. For a moment, Lou considered quietly exiting, and his mind raced with thoughts of running away.

"Forget something else?" his father had asked without turning around.

"No," Lou had responded, feeling cornered. There was no avoiding it now, as his father knew he was in the house. There was nowhere to hide.

"Dad," he had said, his voice breaking. "I—" He couldn't go on. "I—"

He gasped for air and the courage to tell what happened.

"Dad, I—the car—" he stammered as his chest heaved between words. "I think I must have forgotten to set the brake," he blurted. "It's in the river, Dad. The car is in the river! I'm so sorry," he said, bursting into sobs. "I'm so sorry!"

What happened next seared itself so deeply into Lou's memory he was sure that should he ever get Alzheimer's or some similar disease, this would be the last memory to leave him.

He remembered trembling while waiting for his father to respond. His father didn't turn to him but still sat holding the newspaper wide before him. He then slowly reached his left hand to the top corner of the right-hand page and turned it to continue reading. And then he said it, the sentence Lou would never forget. He said, "Well, I guess you'll have to take the truck then."

As Lou remembered this, he sat stunned anew. There had been no retribution, no lecture, no visible anger. Just, "Well, I guess you'll have to take the truck then."

Lou realized in this moment that his father's heart was at peace toward Lou, a peace so powerful that it couldn't be interrupted even by a provocation so great as the sudden loss of a hard-earned car. Perhaps in his wisdom he knew Lou was now the last person who would ever put another car into the river. Perhaps in that instant he divined that a lecture would serve no purpose, and to start one would only hurt an already hurting son.

An already hurting son. Lou reeled at the thought. He had one of those too but had rarely spared the lecture. *What have I become?* he wondered silently. *Why do I turn so quickly to war?*

"I've seen him when he's that way, Yusuf," Carol said, her voice pulling Lou back from the trouble of his thoughts. "I've seen Lou when his heart is at peace. Many times, actually."

Lou turned to her, his mouth opening slightly in grateful surprise.

"Lou can be warm and helpful—despite what you've seen during much of today," she added, apologetically. After a moment's pause, she said, "Can I share a story?"

"Please," nodded Yusuf.

"Before that," she began, "I need to apologize to you, Miguel. It was unkind what I said earlier, about Ria having to do everything. It was terribly inconsiderate and presumptuous of me. I'm so sorry. I hope you can forgive me."

Miguel cleared his throat. "No worries," he smiled. "Forgot all about it."

"Thank you," Carol said. "I'm so sorry."

She turned back to the group. "Okay, so the story," she continued. "This won't be easy for me. I've never shared this with anyone, except Lou and one other person I'll tell you about. But I'm thinking it might be helpful for you—for everyone here—to hear this.

"For years in our marriage," she continued, "I carried a secret. I was bulimic. And I was ashamed about it. I didn't want to let Lou down or to risk losing him or his love. So I never told him. Then something happened that awoke me to the possibility that I might be killing myself—not just emotionally and psychologically but physically as well. I had been severely fatigued for a long time and finally went to see my doctor about it. She ran lots of tests and then asked me point-blank whether I had an eating disorder. At first I denied it. But when she showed me the test results and told me that my body was breaking down and that my health and perhaps even my life was at risk, I finally broke down myself. I told her the truth between sobs.

"But then came the hard part. I knew I had to tell Lou because this problem had morphed way beyond merely a physical ailment. I needed his help, and I couldn't go on keeping such a secret from him daily even if I didn't. So I told him, deathly worried that it might be the beginning of the end of our marriage.

"But it wasn't like that. I think he was hurt by the secret-keeping, but he didn't dwell on it. At least, not that I know of. His concern for me was immediate and overwhelming. I don't think I've ever been so grateful for anyone in my life as I was for him in that moment and the months that followed. We agreed that I would report to him every night about how I had done during the day. There were many days that I had to report meekly to him that I had stumbled. But stumble or not, he gently rubbed my back until I went to sleep. Somewhere amid the back rubs and his nonjudgmental listening to my troubles, my compulsion eventually left me. I haven't even been tempted toward bulimia since that time, which is now many years ago."

As Carol shared her story, the atmosphere in the room began changing. Lou's face, which for much of the morning had been creased with impatience and acrimony, had softened. Carol herself seemed to come alive with a kind of personal conviction and confidence. And finally, Gwyn—Lou's most bitter rival to this point—had relaxed for the first time in an hour. The tension had drained from her face and limbs, and she leaned forward in interest rather than in belligerence. Elizabeth too seemed to be carrying herself differently, her earlier dispassionate air having given way to concentrated attention. She listened intently to Carol.

"Anyway," Carol finished up. "I thought it might help to share that story. He's far from perfect," she said, with a gentle grin, "but fundamentally he's a good man. That's why I wanted to marry him and why I'm still glad about that, despite the challenge we sometimes are for each other."

Lou hung his head a bit. Some might have thought he had tired of attention that in the end must have seemed too effusive for his taste. In reality, however, he was feeling shame. He remembered well the experience Carol had related, but he knew he too rarely lived up to that ideal.

"Thank you, Carol, for sharing that," Yusuf said. "It's a wonderful story. Thank you."

Carol nodded.

"Gwyn," he continued, "I'm curious. What did hearing that story do for you?"

Gwyn was caught off guard by the question and collected herself for a moment before responding. "I'm not sure what you mean."

"Did it influence your impression at all of Lou?"

Gwyn thought about that for a moment. "I suppose it did somewhat, yes."

"Elizabeth?" Yusuf asked. "How about you? Did the story do anything for you?"

Elizabeth looked over at Lou for a moment before responding. "Yes, it did," she said.

"What did it do?"

She looked back at Yusuf. "It reminded me of someone," she answered softly, not volunteering more.

"So do the two of you now think that Lou was right in everything he has said today?"

"No," Gwyn said quickly, but without the edge that had been in her voice before.

"Oh, I don't know that I have been thinking Lou has been entirely wrong," Elizabeth said. "I suppose I've been finding him interesting, let's put it that way."

"I think I'd rather be wrong," Lou joked.

"Yes, well, you haven't been entirely right either," she said.

"That feels much better," Lou cracked.

"So how about you, Lou?" Yusuf asked. "Do you now think that Gwyn has been right, for example, and that you have been wrong?"

"No, sir." The formality surprised everyone, including Lou.

"But when do you think the two of you would be more able to resolve any differences you might have, right now or thirty minutes ago?"

They glanced quickly at each other. "Now, I suppose," Lou answered.

Gwyn nodded in agreement.

"Why is that, do you think?" Yusuf asked. "You still don't agree with the other person's positions, so why do you suppose you'd be more able now than before to find solutions?"

Pettis spoke up. "It's what you and Avi have been talking about: Carol's story humanized Lou, I think. And, I don't know, maybe for Lou, hearing the story with us humanized the group a bit. In your words, I think we're seeing others in the room as people more than we might have been before."

"Exactly," Yusuf agreed. "And that seems to make a difference, doesn't it?"

Pettis and the rest of the group nodded their heads.

"So if we are going to find lasting solutions to difficult conflicts or external wars we find ourselves in," Yusuf said, "we first need to find our way out of the internal wars that are poisoning our thoughts, feelings, and attitudes toward others. If we can't put an end to the violence within us, there is no hope for putting an end to the violence without."

"Then how do you?" Pettis asked.

"In order to understand how to improve our peace," Yusuf answered, "we first must understand how and why we have turned toward war. But it's now past lunchtime."

Everyone in the room looked at their watches almost in unison. They were surprised by the time.

"Let's break for lunch and meet back here at 2:00 p.m. Then we'll get into how our hearts have turned from peace to war. Fair enough?"

"Yes," they all responded.

"One quick thing before you go. While you are out, I challenge you to see everyone you encounter as a person—the driver in the car next to you, the person who waits on you at whatever restaurant you go to, your spouse or partner you are with, and so on. Make a point of seeing everyone over the next ninety minutes as a person and see what happens as a result.

"Fair enough?"

The group, now beginning to stand, nodded.

"Oh, and Teri and Carl," Yusuf called. "Can I talk to you for a moment?"

As Lou was leaving the room, he heard Yusuf say to them, "Your daughter, Jenny—"

"Yes?"

"She's running."

PART II

From Peace to War

8 · *Reality*

"Did you hear that, Carol?" Lou said chasing after her out
to the parking lot. "That girl, Jenny—you know, the one who
was yelling and carrying on this morning—she took off running."

"Where?"

"Here, out in the streets. She just took off running across
town."

Carol stopped. "Oh, how terrible," she said, looking up the
street. "Poor girl. She wasn't wearing any shoes. Do you think
we should try to find her?"

"I'm sure Yusuf and his team are handling it," he said.

Before now, Carol would have thought this a sarcastic dig,
but she thought she heard a hint of respect in Lou's voice.

Lou glanced at his watch. "Listen, Carol, I have to make
some calls."

"Now?"

"Yes. The situation at the office is kind of a mess. I have to
check in with a couple of people."

"Can't you do that later?"

"They'll probably be gone home by the time we're out this
evening. I'm going to have to call now."

"You never worried about calling them at home on Friday
nights before," she said, coyly. "Why now?"

Lou knew what Carol was searching for, but he didn't want
her to have the satisfaction of knowing he was actually considering what Avi and Yusuf had said. Avoiding a direct answer to

her question, he said, "Well, I'd rather not call them at home if I can help it. Not with all the turmoil everyone's in. Don't want to add to it, I suppose."

"Okay," Carol said. "I'll bring you back something to eat."

"Thanks," Lou said as he turned to look for a private place to make his calls.

He knew whom he needed to call first: his secretary. But he got her voice mail. *Where is she!* he thought, before catching himself.

"Please leave me a message," came the pleasant voice.

"Susan, it's Lou. Just checking in for a report. I'll try you later." In that moment, he suddenly flashed back to the blustery way he'd left the office the day before and felt a tinge of regret. "Oh, and one more thing," he found himself saying. "I'm, uh—" he hesitated. "I'm sorry for blowing up at you yesterday on the way out of town. I didn't mean it, really. I think I was just feeling the load of all that's going on, and I ended up taking it out on you. So, sorry about that. Anyway, that's all. Carry on."

"*Carry on*"? Lou repeated as he hung up the phone. *You can't do any better than that? "Carry on"?* Lou shook his head. *Wow, once 'Nam's in your system, you just can't shake it.*

Other than feeling a bit of chagrin over his military-issue good-bye, Lou felt good having made the call to Susan.

But the next call was going to be harder. It was to Kate— Kate Stenarude, who had led the mutiny of his executive staff.

Kate had been one of the original twenty employees at Zagrum, where she started as an order fulfillment clerk after graduating from college with a degree in history. It turns out she had been a brilliant hire, as her combination of brains, likability, and professional drive quickly elevated her to the top of the sales division. Despite her young age, until the March Meltdown she had been everyone's pick as Lou's successor—if and when he ever decided to retire, that is. This love for her was partly born of a desperate hope as she was the single person who while possessing the business vision and smarts required to run the operation also retained a deeply felt appreciation for the people around her, regardless of rank or position. When she walked in the Zagrum doors each morning as Zagrum's director of sales, she walked and talked and greeted and laughed the same way she did the day she was hired. She walked in not as a big shot but as one of the people. And the people loved her for it.

So when she walked out of the building on that rainy Connecticut March morning, "escorted" on Lou's command by apologetic members of the security staff, it was as though the company's heart and soul walked out with her. Lou knew this, although until now he had been trying to deny the full impact of her leaving. But the truth was her loss hurt the company more than the loss of the other four executives combined. And probably more, even, than if Lou had left himself.

He had to call her. *But what am I going to say?* he wondered.

He stood there with the clumsy uncertainty he once felt as a teenager when he was trying to motivate himself to call and ask a girl out.

Ah hell, just call her! he shouted internally, calling himself out of his adolescent timidity.

He dialed the number and waited: one ring, then two, three, four.

With each ring he felt the youthful panic build again within him until he was telling himself that if she didn't pick up by ring six, he would hang up.

The sixth ring hadn't even completed before he terminated the call, a spasm of relief releasing droplets of sweat on his brow. *Well, I tried,* he said to himself. *I'll catch her later.*

But his racing heart told him that he might not get the courage up to do it again for days. If ever.

Now for real work, he thought to himself, as he dialed up John Rencher, the president of the local union, who was threatening a strike.

"Hello?" came the voice.

"John." It was more of a summons to attention than a greeting.

"Yes."

"It's Lou Herbert."

Silence.

Just then Lou thought of Yusuf's assignment to see everyone as people.

"Hey, listen, John," he said, in as kind a voice as he could muster, "I was wondering if we could get together when I get back and take another look at your proposal."

"Take another look at it yourself," Rencher shot back. "You've had it for a week."

"I just thought you and I could get further if we talked things over," Lou responded, still as agreeably as he could.

"So you still want more from us."

"Well, this is a negotiation after all."

"No, Lou, this is an ultimatum. We're going to shut you down until you meet our demands. You've railroaded our people for too long. It's over, Lou."

"Now you listen here, you little scumbag," Lou exploded. "You can take your clock-watching, do-nothing morons and go ruin someone else's company if you want. But if you walk out on me, you're over at Zagrum. The union will never walk through my doors again. You got that?"

"You got that?" he repeated.

"I said, *you got that!*"

But the line was dead. Rencher had hung up.

Lou bellowed in frustration as he flung the phone at the wall. "Stupid homework," he muttered. "See people as people," he repeated to himself sarcastically in a sing-song tone. "What a joke. Yusuf hasn't worked a day in the real world. He doesn't know squat! Yeah, go ahead Yusi," he said to the air mockingly, "try your little soft-pop stuff on the union. Yeah, that'll work. And on the terrorists. And on Cory too. Sure, they'll all just roll over and pant happily after receiving a little of your Middle Eastern love." He laughed at the oxymoronic ring to this and then shook his head, half out of anger, half out of disgust. "What a waste. This whole thing is a waste."

When Carol returned from lunch, a take-out box for Lou in her hand, Lou intercepted her before she entered the building.

"Carol, we're leaving."

"What?" she uttered in complete surprise.

"You heard me, we're leaving."

"Leaving," she repeated in disbelief. "Why?"

"Because this is a waste of time, and I don't have time to waste."

Carol looked at him warily. "What happened on your calls, Lou?"

"Nothing."

"Seriously, Lou, what happened?"

"Okay, I'll tell you, if you really want to know. I was yanked back to reality, that's what happened. Someone brought me back to my senses. Come on. We're going."

At that, Lou started for the car.

But Carol didn't budge.

"Carol, I said we're leaving."

"I know what you said, but I won't allow it. Not this time, Lou. The stakes are too high."

"You're damn right the stakes are too high, Carol. That's why we have to go."

"No, Lou, that's why we have to stay. The stakes you're worried about, whatever they are, are high because of how we've been mostly tone-deaf to what we're starting to learn here. I'm not leaving, Lou.

"Okay, have it your way, Carol," he said, dismissing her with a quick flick of his wrist. "*I'm* leaving then."

Carol stood in silence. The hope that had developed within her through the morning was now fading. *See him as a person, see him as a person,* she repeated within. *You've got to keep seeing him as a person.*

"Lou—"

He stopped and turned to her. "Yeah?"

"If you leave here, Honey," she said, "I'll leave you."

"You'll what?"

In this moment, Carol was struck by how much she loved this man. Despite his belligerence, she was not raging within toward him. And his bullheadedness did not wash from her memory the many wonderful things he had done for her and for others. He wasn't a saint, to be sure, but there were times—especially during some of the private moments that make up most of life—that he cared and loved and acted in saintly ways. He was better in private than he was in the glare of public moments, which was just the opposite of many people she knew. And it seemed to her that his brand of private strength and public weakness showed more goodness and character than those who hid private weakness with conjured public strength. *Yes,* she thought to herself, *I'd take him again if we had the chance to do everything over.*

So she was surprised when she heard herself say again, "I'll leave you, Lou. And I mean it."

Lou stood for a moment in complete silence. Every muscle in his body had frozen still, as if afraid to move for where the movement might lead.

"Carol," he said finally, almost pleading, "you can't be serious."

Carol nodded slightly. "Yes, Lou, I'm afraid I am.

"Don't misunderstand," she added. "I don't want to leave you. But I will."

This knocked Lou completely out of sorts.

"Listen, Lou, I think we need this. I think Cory needs it from us. And I think we need it for him and for each other. You might need it for Zagrum too," she added. "And for Kate."

This last mention of Kate caught Lou, for it took him back to the feeling he had when he knew he needed to call her, which seemed like years ago.

He slumped his shoulders and heaved a heavy sigh.

"Okay, Carol," he said, forlornly. "You win. I'll stay."

Then he paused. "But only until tonight."

9 • *The Beginning of an Idea*

Lou picked at the Mexican food Carol had brought him while the group assembled back into the room. The mood was much lighter among them than it had been at the beginning, when they were sizing each other up. And the tension that had filled the interchange during much of the morning session seemed to have faded away. Gwyn, in fact, was deep in conversation with Miguel and seemed to be enjoying it. Elizabeth and Carol were in the back of the room browsing a Camp Moriah leaflet together.

Just then, Pettis walked up to Lou from behind.

"So, Lou," he said, as if they were just picking up on a conversation that had been recently interrupted, "four years in 'Nam."

Lou nodded.

"Hat's off to you, my friend. I was there, but it's different flying above the jungle than it was down below. I know that."

Lou nodded appreciatively. In peacetime, pilots always think themselves superior to the so-called grunts on the ground. And the infantrymen carry around an inferiority complex about it as well, although they'd never admit it. In wartime, however, the psychology changes. The high-flying pilots quickly develop a deep admiration for their partners on the ground. And soldiers on the ground, although grateful for their cover when they hear the roar of supportive aircraft overhead, would tell you, if pressed, that those well-heeled flyboys never get their uniforms dirty enough or their vital parts close enough to the crosshairs of the enemy to know real bravery—or fear for that matter. In Vietnam and elsewhere, the grunts receive the lion's share of the admiration and respect of fellow soldiers.

"Thanks, Pettis. It's good to be with a fellow vet. Tell me," he continued, "what is it you do in Texas?"

Five minutes or so later, Avi and Yusuf walked in the room, and everyone, Lou and Pettis included, took their seats. Lou looked across at Jenny's parents who appeared to be okay, a surprise to him under the circumstances.

"Well, welcome back," Avi greeted them. "Before we move forward, does anyone have any questions about anything?"

Lou shot his hand up—the first time he hadn't just blurted out a comment. "What happened to Jenny?"

"Jenny is fine," Yusuf answered. "As some of you may know," he continued, "she took off running soon after we started this morning."

"Have you caught her?" Lou followed up.

"Actually, Lou, we're not trying to catch her," Yusuf answered. "This is a voluntary program, so we won't force anyone into it. But we will make sure she stays safe. And we'll do that in a way that invites her, as much as possible, to choose to join with us."

Lou was perplexed. "So what does that mean you're doing?" he asked.

"It means two of our workers are following her, trying to engage her in meaningful conversation, and a truck with backup if needed is following behind but out of sight. Everything will be fine," he smiled. "Anything else?"

Lou raised his hand again.

"This whole 'see people as people or see them as objects' distinction," he said with a hint of disdain in his voice, "where does it come from?"

Avi spoke first. "It comes out of an exploration in philosophy," he said. "Perhaps it would help to give a brief overview." He looked over at Yusuf, who nodded.

Avi turned back to the group. "I hesitate doing philosophy with you," he said with an apologetic smirk. "Especially first thing after lunch. But I'll take a chance on it, for a minute or two anyway. If you're pretty sure you don't want any philosophy, just plug your ears for a minute." He looked around the room. "You are all familiar with the philosopher René Descartes?"

"Not a bad philosopher—for a Frenchman," Elizabeth cracked. Her hands were no longer clasped together, and she was leaning back comfortably in her chair.

"Not bad indeed," Avi grinned. Turning to the rest, he continued. "Descartes is the father of what is known as the modern period of philosophy, and he is famous still to this day for the starting point of his very ambitious philosophical theory, which he hoped would explain all of existence. His foundational assumption was the famous line *Cogito ergo sum*—or, 'I think therefore I am.'"

Familiarity shown in the eyes of most in the room.

"You will notice there are big assumptions in Descartes' starting point," Avi continued. "The biggest of these is the assumption of the primacy of the separate human consciousness— what Descartes called the *I*.

"Hundreds of years after Descartes, a series of philosophers began to call into question the modern philosophical arguments that Descartes started in motion, in particular this central individualistic assumption that undergirded Descartes' work. One of these philosophers was a man named Martin Heidegger. If Heidegger had been a contemporary of Descartes, he might have asked him this question: 'René, tell me—from where did you acquire the language that enabled you to formulate the thought "I think therefore I am"?'"

Avi looked around the group to let that question settle on them. "Of course," he continued, "Descartes acquired those words, and the ability to think with them, from others. Which is to say, he did not conjure them from a separate, individualized I.

"Consider what this means for Descartes' theory," he continued. "There is a kind of brute fact that just is—the fact of *being in the world with others*. Descartes was able to postulate that the separate self was what was most fundamental only because he acquired language in a world *with others*."

"Ah," Elizabeth interjected, "so being in the world with others, and not the idea of a separate self, is what is fundamental. Is that what you are suggesting?"

"Exactly," Avi agreed. "Descartes' foundational assumption is disproved by the conditions that made it possible for him to state it in the first place. So Heidegger, among others," he continued, "with his attack on individualism, shifted the focus of the philosophical world away from the separate self and onto the idea of being with others.

"A contemporary of Heidegger named Martin Buber, whom I mentioned this morning, agreed with Heidegger that way of being in the world is what is most fundamental to human experience. He observed that there are basically two ways of being in the world: we can be in the world seeing others as people or we can be in the world seeing others as objects. He called the first way of being the I-Thou way and the second the I-It way, and he argued that we are always, in every moment, being either I-Thou or I-It—seeing others as people or seeing others as objects.

"So, Lou," he said, turning to face him, "that is a long way of saying that it was Martin Buber who first observed these two basic ways of being, or at least formulated them that way. He was the first to articulate the differences in human experience when we are seeing others as objects as opposed to seeing them as they are, as people." Looking around at the rest of the group, he said, "Okay, it's safe to unplug your ears now."

"Well, almost," Yusuf interjected with a smile. "Let me add one more thought. Buber's observation of these two ways of being raised the question of how we move from one way of being to another—from seeing people as people, for example, to seeing others as objects, and vice versa. But this is a question Buber never answered. He simply observed the two ways of being and their differences. It is left to us, now, to figure out how we can change our way of being—if we want to, that is.

"For our purposes," he continued, "the question Buber did not address is the question we must answer. We have been suggesting that the foundational problem in our homes, our workplaces, and our battlefields is that our hearts are too often at war—that is, we too often insist on seeing people as objects. And we have seen how one warring heart invites more 'object-seeing' and war in others. It follows from this that in order to find peace, we must first understand how we and others have foregone peace and chosen war."

"Sometimes we don't choose war," Lou butted in. "Rather, it chooses us."

"Yes, Lou," Yusuf agreed. "Sometimes we might be forced to defend ourselves, you're exactly right. But that is a different thing than saying that we are forced to despise, to rage, to denigrate, to belittle. No one can force a warring heart upon us. When our hearts go to war, we ourselves have chosen it."

"How?" Lou asked.

"That is exactly what we will now explore," Yusuf answered.

10 · Choosing War

"I was raised," Yusuf began, "in a village of rock-walled homes in the hills on the western edge of Jerusalem. The village, called Deir Yassin, had been my family's home for at least two centuries. But that all ended early on the morning of April 9, 1948, at the height of the Arab-Jewish fighting surrounding the establishment of Israel. I was just five years old at the time. I remember being awakened by shouting and gunfire. Our village was being attacked by what I later learned were members of a Jewish underground military group. My father grabbed me from bed and thrust me and my two sisters into my parents' room. He then pulled a rifle from under his mattress and, pulling on his boots, ran out of the house. 'Stay inside!' he yelled to us. 'Don't come out for anyone, you hear? Until I return, God willing.'

"Those were the last words I ever heard my father speak. When it was over and we left the protection of our stone walls, bodies and exploded body parts littered the streets. My father was among the dead."

"How terrible," Ria said.

"It was many years ago," Yusuf responded. "Those days and the years that followed were difficult for me and my family, I won't deny it. But we weren't the only ones that suffered tragedy."

Elizabeth spoke up. "I was going to say, I have some Jewish friends that have similar stories to tell."

"I'm sure you do," Yusuf said, "as do I. A Jewish village called Kfar Etzion was attacked by Arab forces at around the same time, for example. The entire village was basically massacred, so I can hardly say that my fate was worse than theirs. By telling my story, I did not mean to imply that Arabs are the only ones that have suffered unjustly. I'm sorry if it seemed that way. Avi's father, for example, was killed while defending his country against an Arab attack. That hurt him as much as losing my father hurt me. Over the years and centuries, violence has been hurled hatefully in all directions. That is the tragic, bloody truth."

Lou was glad to hear Yusuf own up to Arab atrocities, but he felt uneasy all the same. It seemed to Lou that Yusuf was too quick to equate Arab and Israeli suffering when in Lou's mind the scales of unjustified suffering clearly leaned in the Israeli direction. Lou wasn't sure, but he thought he might have an ally in this belief in Elizabeth Wingfield.

"After my father died," Yusuf continued, "my mother moved us from village to village until we finally found refuge in Jordan, or what was then called Transjordan. We settled in a refugee camp in a town called Zarqa, which is on the northwest side of the city of Amman. When Jordan annexed the West Bank following the War of 1948, known in Israel as the War of Independence, my mother moved us back to the west side of the Jordan River. We moved to the town of Bethlehem, which is only a few miles from Deir Yassin.

"As I look back now, and put myself in my mother's place, it was bold of her to return so close to the place of her personal tragedy. Years later she told me that she felt compelled to return as close to her roots as she could. We took up residence in Bethlehem with her sister—my aunt, Asima.

"The economy of Bethlehem, such as it was, depended largely on Christians who made pilgrimages to the historical birthplace of Jesus. The war severely reduced the number of visitors, so merchants were hard up for customers. I was hired as a street hustler at the age of eight. My job was to make Westerners feel sorry for me and then lead them to the shops of the people who had hired me. In broken English, I began to interact with the West.

"As for the Jews, I had little opportunity or desire to interact with them. The Jews had been expelled from the West Bank after Jordan annexed it. Border penetrations from both directions, whether for military or economic reasons, usually ended in gunfire and casualties. The Jews were our enemies.

"At least, this is the simplistic picture most often recited and remembered. The truth was a bit more nuanced. I know because I worked the same streets as a certain blind Jewish man, appealing to the same Western wallets for the same Western money.

"Which brings me to the story I want to share with you. I had come to know this man, Mordechai Lavon, at what you might call a close distance. We often worked the streets within mere feet of each other, and although I was well acquainted with his voice and he with mine, I had never once addressed him, even though he tried to strike up a conversation on occasion.

"One day, he stumbled as he asked a passerby for help. His purse burst open as it hit the ground, and his coins flew in all directions into the street.

"As his hands groped first for his purse and then in search of the individual coins, I had a sudden thought. You might call it a sense of something to do, something I knew in that instant was the right thing to do. I think it would be accurate, in fact, to call it a desire. That is, I felt a desire to help him—first to help him to his feet and then to retrieve his coins for him.

"I had a choice, of course. I could act on this sense I had, or I could resist it. Which do you suppose I did?"

"I'd imagine you helped," Carol said.

"No he didn't," Lou smirked. "He wouldn't be telling the story if he had."

Yusuf smiled. "True enough, Lou. You're right. I resisted the sense I had to help Mordechai. A stronger way to say it is that I betrayed that sense and acted contrary to what I knew was right in that moment. Instead of helping, I turned and walked the other way.

"As I was walking away," he said to the group, "what sorts of things do you suppose I might have started to say and think to myself about Mordechai Lavon?"

"That he shouldn't have been there anyway," Gwyn responded. "You and the rest of your neighbors were kind to allow him to stay. After all, he was one of the enemy, who robbed you of your peace. A "Zionist threat. A bigot."

"Now," Elizabeth began, in a puzzled voice, "who was the bigot?"

"I'm not saying Mordechai was a bigot," Gwyn answered.

"Neither am I," Elizabeth agreed.

"Oh, I see," Gwyn said. "I'm the bigot, then. Is that what you're saying?"

"I don't know, I was just asking," Elizabeth said, coolly.

"Look, Elizabeth, Mordechai may or may not have been a bigot. Who knows? I'm just saying that Yusuf probably saw him that way, and his people too. That's all. Is that a problem?"

"Not at all. Thank you," Elizabeth said as she looked down at her lap and straightened a crease in her skirt.

"Sure. And thank you to the Brits for dividing Mordechai's and Yusuf's lands in the first place. With a little help from the French, of course. That helped a lot."

The air was suddenly electric. Lou leaned forward to get a good look at what would happen next.

Elizabeth didn't say anything for a moment. "History has certainly called those events into question, hasn't it?' she finally said, with no hint of venom in her voice. "Sorry to have tweaked you with the bigot remark, my dear. It was a bit forward. I'd say it was almost American of me, but that would expose me too fully, wouldn't it?" She smiled demurely.

The charge seemed to leave the air as quickly as it had come.

"No, we wouldn't want to be American now, would we?" Gwyn smiled.

"Heaven forbid," Elizabeth cracked.

"For a moment, I thought I might have to put Lou between the two of you," Yusuf said, eliciting a roar of laughter from the group.

"What's so funny?" Lou deadpanned.

Amid the laughter, Yusuf wrote, "No right to be there," "Robs me of peace," "Zionist threat," and "Bigot" to summarize the ways he was seeing Mordechai.

"Okay then," Yusuf said after he finished writing, "if I was starting to see Mordechai in these ways we've mentioned, how do you suppose I might have started to see myself?"

"As a victim," Pettis answered.

"And as better than he was," Gwyn said.

"I don't know," Carol spoke up, "you might have gotten down on yourself—like you weren't good enough. Deep down, I think you would have felt like you weren't being a very good person."

"Maybe so," Gwyn agreed, "but it wasn't his fault, after everything that had happened. If he was bad, it was because of what others had done to him."

"I don't know," Lou disagreed. "That sounds like a cop-out."

"We'll get to whether it's a cop-out," Yusuf stepped in. "But I think what Gwyn said certainly describes what I was at least believing to be the case at the time."

"Okay," Lou allowed.

"What else?" Yusuf asked.

"I'm thinking about how you walked away after you noticed the coins," Pettis answered. "On the one hand, I can see how a feeling of victimization would invite you to walk away. But I think there could have been another motivation as well."

"Go on," Yusuf invited.

"Well," Pettis responded, "I'm thinking that by turning quickly away, you were giving yourself an excuse. Your turn away might have been out of a need to be seen as a good person."

"What do you mean?" Lou asked. "If he turned away, how does that make him a good person?"

"It doesn't," Pettis answered. "But it makes it easier for him to *claim* that he is. If he didn't need to be seen as being good, he could have just stood and watched Mordechai struggle. But by quickly turning away so it seemed like he didn't see the situation, he preserved his reputation—his claim of goodness."

Yusuf started to chuckle. "That's a really interesting insight, Pettis. It reminds me of something that happened just this morning. I was making myself a sandwich, and I noticed that I'd dropped a piece of lettuce on the floor. It would have been easy to bend over and pick it up, but I didn't. Instead, I pushed it under the counter with my toe! I wouldn't have had to do that unless I was concerned with showing my wife, Lina, that I was a good person—tidy, responsible, and so on. Otherwise, I might have just left it there."

"Well why not just pick it up?" Gwyn objected. "Honestly!"

"Yes," Yusuf agreed. "And why not just pick up the coins too? That's exactly the question we're beginning to explore."

At that he added "Want to be seen well" to the list he was constructing on the board.

"Okay then," he said, as he turned back to the group. "When I'm seeing this man and myself in the ways we've discussed, how do you suppose I might have viewed the circumstances I found myself in?"

"As unfair," Gwyn answered.

Yusuf started writing that on the board.

"And unjust," added Ria.

"And burdensome," said Pettis. "Given all you'd suffered, I can imagine you went around feeling angry or depressed."

"Yes," Elizabeth agreed. "In fact, you might have felt that the whole world was lined up against you—against your happiness, against your security, against your well-being."

"Excellent. Thank you," Yusuf said as he finished writing. "Now, I'd like to play off something Pettis just said—that I might have felt angry or depressed. Can you think of any other ways I might have felt given the way I was seeing everything else?"

"You would have been bitter," Gwyn answered.

"Okay, excellent," Yusuf said, adding "Bitter" to "Angry" and "Depressed" on the diagram. "But if you were to ask me why I was feeling those ways, what do you think I would have said?"

"That it wasn't your fault," Pettis answered. "You would have said it was the Israelis' fault—that you felt that way only because of what they had done to you and your people."

"Yes, Pettis, I think that is what I would have said," Yusuf agreed. "Which is to say that I felt justified in my anger, my depression, and my bitterness. I felt justified in my judgmental view of Mordechai. However I was feeling or reacting, I felt caused to feel and react that way, didn't I?"

At this, he added the word "Justified" to the diagram. "That's what my entire experience here was telling me," he said, pointing at the board. "That I didn't do anything wrong, and that others were to blame. That is what I was believing, was it not?"

View of Myself	View of Mordechai
Better than	No right to be there
A victim (so owed)	Robs me of peace
Bad (but made to be)	Zionist threat
Want to be seen well	Bigot
Feelings	**View of World**
Angry	Unfair
Depressed	Unjust
Bitter	Burdensome
Justified	Against me

"Yes," Pettis answered, giving voice to the prevailing thought in the room. "That's what you were believing."

"That I wasn't responsible for how I was seeing and feeling?" Yusuf followed up.

"Yes."

"But is that true?" Yusuf asked. "Was I really caused by outside forces to see and feel in these ways—the way I believed when I was in this box here? Or was I rather choosing to see and feel in these ways?"

"You're suggesting you were actually choosing to be angry, depressed, and bitter?" Gwyn asked incredulously.

"I'm suggesting I was making a choice that resulted in my feeling angry, depressed, and bitter. A choice that was my choice, and no one else's—not Mordechai's, not the Israelis'."

Yusuf looked around at a room full of perplexed faces. "Perhaps it would help," he said, "to put the diagram in context." He then added the following:

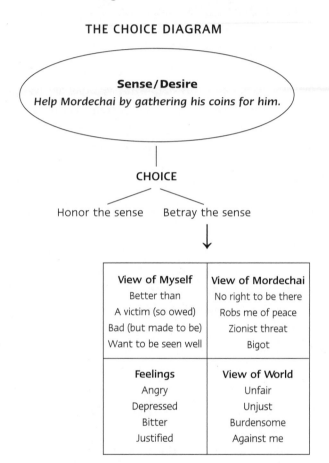

THE CHOICE DIAGRAM

Sense/Desire
Help Mordechai by gathering his coins for him.

CHOICE

Honor the sense   Betray the sense

View of Myself	View of Mordechai
Better than	No right to be there
A victim (so owed)	Robs me of peace
Bad (but made to be)	Zionist threat
Want to be seen well	Bigot
Feelings	**View of World**
Angry	Unfair
Depressed	Unjust
Bitter	Burdensome
Justified	Against me

"As you'll recall," he began, "this is exactly what happened: I had a sense or desire to help Mordechai in this moment. It was my sense, my desire. I knew it was the right thing to do. But this then presented a choice: I could either honor my sense to help or I could betray it and choose not to help. Which is to say that we don't always do what we know is the right thing to do, do we?"

The group looked uncertain.

"For example," Yusuf continued, "We don't always apologize when we know we should, do we?"

Lou thought of the apology he still owed Kate.

"When a spouse or child or neighbor is struggling with something we could easily help with, we don't always offer that help. Don't we sometimes persist in sitting on the couch and watching television, for example, instead of getting up and helping the person who is struggling to clean the kitchen?"

Lou wasn't much for television, but he knew he hadn't washed nearly as many dishes during his married life as Carol had. Had he felt he should? Had he made a choice not to? He wasn't sure.

"And don't we sometimes hold onto information we know we should share with others?" Yusuf continued. "At work, for example, when we know a piece of information would help a coworker, don't we sometimes hold it for ourselves?"

Most in the group nodded their heads contemplatively, including Lou, who knew this scenario well.

"Sometimes we do what we know to be the right thing in the moment," Yusuf said, shrugging his shoulders, "and sometimes we don't. That's a statement of the obvious, of course, but it reveals the presence of a choice, doesn't it?"

Again, the heads around the room nodded in agreement.

"When I choose to act contrary to my own sense of what is appropriate," Yusuf continued, "I commit what we at Camp Moriah call an act of self-betrayal. It is a betrayal of my own sense of the right way to act in a given moment in time—not someone else's sense or standard, but what I myself feel is right in the moment.

"Acts of self-betrayal such as those I've mentioned are so common they are almost ho-hum. But when we dig a little deeper, we discover something fascinating about self-betrayal."

He looked around at the group. "A choice to betray myself," he said, "is a choice to go to war."

11 · A Need for War

"How is a choice to betray oneself a choice to go to war?" Lou asked, troubled by the claim.

"Because when I betray myself," Yusuf answered, "I create within myself a new need—a need that causes me to see others accusingly, a need that causes me to care about something other than truth and solutions, and a need that invites others to do the same in response."

"What need is that?" Pettis asked.

Yusuf turned back to the choice diagram. "At the beginning here, when I had the desire to help Mordechai, how would you say I was seeing him? Was he a person or an object to me?"

The group collectively murmured, "He was a person."

"How about down here at the end, when I was in this box. Was he still a person to me then?"

They looked at the diagram.

Pettis spoke up. "No, you'd dehumanized him. He's almost a caricature."

"So what was he to me at that point, a person or an object?"

"An object," Pettis answered.

"Which gives rise to what need?" Yusuf asked.

Pettis and the others puzzled over that. "I'm not sure what you mean," he said.

"At the end of this story, when I was seeing Mordechai as an object, I had a need for something—something I had no need for at the beginning of the story, when I was seeing him as a person. What did I now need?"

Still, the group sat in silence.

"Look at the diagram," Yusuf invited. "The answer is on the diagram."

After a moment, he said, "Perhaps an analogy would help. My father was a carpenter. When I was four or five, I remember going with him on a job where he was helping to rebuild a house. I remember in particular a wall in the kitchen area of the home. It turned out that the wall was crooked. I remember this because of something my father taught me about it. 'Here, Yusuf,' I remember him saying, although in Arabic, of course, 'we need to justify this wall.'

"'Justify, Father?' I asked.

"'Yes, Son. When something is crooked and we need to make it straight, we call it justifying. This wall is crooked, so it needs to be justified.'"

With that, Yusuf looked around at the group.

"With that story as an analogy," he said, "take another look at the diagram."

Carol's quiet voice came in immediate reply. "You needed to be justified in the story," she said. "That's the need you're talking about, isn't it?"

"Yes, Carol," Yusuf smiled, "it is. And did I have any need to be justified when I had the desire to help Mordechai?"

"No."

"Why not?"

"Because you weren't being crooked toward him in that moment."

"Exactly," Yusuf agreed, landing heavily and happily on the word. "Did everyone catch that?" he asked the group.

Heads nodded around the room, but not convincingly enough for Yusuf's taste.

"Let's be really clear on this," he said. "What was crooked when I turned my back on Mordechai that wasn't crooked before?"

"Your view of him," Carol answered.

"Yes," Yusuf agreed. "And what was crooked about that view of him?"

"You weren't seeing him as a person any longer," Pettis answered. "He didn't count any more. At least not like you counted."

"Exactly. In fact, it was precisely *because* I was seeing him as a person at the beginning of the story that I wanted to help him. But the moment I began to violate the basic call of his humanity upon me, I created within me a new need, a need that didn't exist the moment before; I needed to be justified for violating the truth I knew in that moment—that he was as human and legitimate as I was.

"Having violated this truth, my entire perception now raced to make me justified. Think about it. When do you suppose Mordechai's personal quirks, whatever they might have been, seemed larger to me, before I betrayed my sense to help him, or after?"

"After," the group answered.

"And when do you suppose the group I lumped Mordechai in with, the Israelis, seemed worse to me? In the moment I had the sense to help Mordechai, or after I failed to help him?"

"After," the group repeated.

"So notice," Yusuf continued, "when I betray myself, others' faults become immediately inflated in my heart and mind. I begin to 'horribilize' others. That is, I begin to make them out to be worse than they really are. And I do this because the worse they are, the more justified I feel. A needy man on the street suddenly represents a threat to my very peace and freedom. A person to help becomes an object to blame."

At this, Yusuf turned to the board and added to the diagram they were discussing. As he was finishing, Gwyn asked, "But what if Mordechai really was a problem? What if he wasn't some gentle blind man but an out-and-out racist jerk? What if he outwardly agreed with the people who had thrust your family from your home? Wouldn't you be justified in that case?"

"What need would I have to be justified if I wasn't somehow crooked?" Yusuf asked, turning from the board to face the group.

Gwyn was clearly frustrated by that answer. "I'm sorry, Yusuf," she said, "but I don't know if I can accept that. It seems like you're just giving bad people a pass."

Yusuf's eyes seemed to soften at this comment. "I appreciate how seriously you are grappling with this, Gwyn," he said. "I am wondering if you would be willing to grapple with another question just as seriously."

"Maybe," she answered pensively.

Yusuf smiled. Being reflexively cynical himself, he appreciated those who listened with a healthy dose of careful skepticism. "You are worried that I might be giving Mordechai a pass, that I might not be holding him accountable for wrongs he or his clan have perpetrated. Am I right?"

Gwyn nodded. "Yes."

"There is a question I have learned to ask myself, Gwyn, when I am feeling bothered about others: am I holding myself to the same standard I am demanding of them? In other words, if I am worried that others are getting a pass, am I also worried about whether I am giving myself one? Am I as vigilant in demanding the eradication of my own bigotry as I am in demanding the eradication of theirs?"

He paused a moment to let that settle.

"If I'm not, I will be living in a kind of fog that obscures all the reality around and within me. Like a pilot in a cloud bank whose senses are telling him just the opposite of what his instrument panel is saying, my senses will be systematically lying to me—about myself, about others, and about my circumstances." Focusing clearly on Gwyn and capturing her gaze, he added, "My Mordechais may not be as prejudiced as I think they are."

"Yours may not be," Gwyn challenged him. "I wouldn't know. But mine are."

Yusuf looked thoughtfully at Gwyn. "You may be right," he said, a touch of resignation in his voice. "Your Mordechais might be prejudiced. Some people are, after all. And to the larger point, you might have suffered some terrible mistreatments at others' hands. All of you who are parents here, for example," he said, looking around the semicircle, "have undoubtedly been treated terribly at times—unjustly, unfairly, ungratefully. Right?"

Heads nodded.

"And you may have been railroaded at work as well— blamed, overlooked, unappreciated. Or perhaps you have been mistreated by society generally. Maybe you belong to a religion that you feel is treated prejudicially, or to an ethnic group that you feel is systematically disenfranchised, or to a class that is ignored or despised. I know a thing or two about each of these mistreatments. I know what they feel like, and I know how terrible they are. I can say from experience that there are few things so painful as contempt from others."

"That's right," Gwyn readily agreed. Others nodded as well.

"Few things except one," Yusuf continued. "As painful as it is to receive contempt from another, it is more debilitating by far to be filled with contempt for another. In this too I speak from painful experience. My own contempt for others is the most debilitating pain of all, for when I am in the middle of it— when I'm seeing resentfully and disdainfully—I condemn myself to living in a disdained, resented world.

"Which brings me back to Mordechai," he said. "Would you say I was filled with resentment or contempt when I had the sense to help him?"

The group looked back at the diagram.

THE CHOICE DIAGRAM

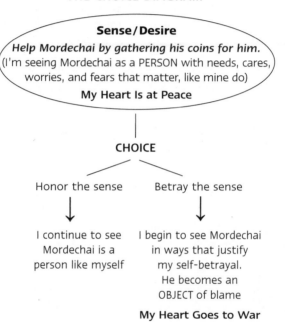

Sense/Desire

Help Mordechai by gathering his coins for him.
(I'm seeing Mordechai as a PERSON with needs, cares, worries, and fears that matter, like mine do)

My Heart Is at Peace

CHOICE

Honor the sense   Betray the sense

I continue to see Mordechai is a person like myself

I begin to see Mordechai in ways that justify my self-betrayal. He becomes an OBJECT of blame

My Heart Goes to War

View of Myself	View of Mordechai
Better than	No right to be there
A victim (so owed)	Robs me of peace
Bad (but made to be)	Zionist threat
Want to be seen well	Bigot
Feelings	**View of World**
Angry	Unfair
Depressed	Unjust
Bitter	Burdensome
Justified	Against me

"No," Ria answered, followed by the others saying the same thing.

"But how about at the end of the story," Yusuf asked, "when I was down in this box seeing him as a bigot and Zionist threat? Was I feeling resentful then?"

The group looked at the feelings that were listed in the box: angry, depressed, bitter, justified. "Yes," they nodded.

"So why was I feeling that way?" Yusuf asked. "I had certainly suffered my share of hardships. Was that the cause of my bitterness, my anger, my resentment, and my contempt?"

"Probably," Gwyn answered.

"Look at the diagram again," Yusuf said.

"No," Pettis answered, "your hardships did not cause your feelings."

"Why do you say that?" Yusuf asked.

"Because whatever hardships you had suffered you had already suffered at the beginning of this story. But those hardships didn't prevent you from seeing Mordechai as a person when you felt the desire to help him with his coins."

"Exactly," Yusuf said. "So what's the only thing that happened between the time at the beginning of this story when I wasn't feeling angry and bitter and the time at the end when I was? What's the only thing that happened between the time that I saw Mordechai as a person and the time I saw him as an object?"

"Your choice to betray yourself," Pettis answered.

"So what was the cause of my anger, my bitterness, my resentment, my contempt, my lack of peace? Was it Mordechai and his people? Or was it me?"

"Well, the diagram says it was you," Lou answered.

"But you're not convinced."

"No, I'm not sure that I am," Lou said. "Look, isn't it possible you simply had a momentary lapse of memory when the coins spilled from Mordechai's purse, a moment when your hardships weren't foremost on your mind? It seems to me that's what likely happened. And then a moment later you came back to reality and remembered all the trouble you'd suffered at the hands of the Israelis. It's not like your bitterness just started in this moment. You'd felt it before. And you might have felt it, like Gwyn said, because of what the Israelis had done to you and your family."

"What, you're siding with me now?" Gwyn asked in jest.

"I know. It has me worried too," Lou smirked.

Yusuf smiled. "That's a great question, Lou. You're right, of course, that this wasn't the first time I had felt angry and bitter toward the Israelis. And you are right as well when you imply that my father's death, and the hardships it caused my family, certainly played a role. But I believe it played a different role than the one you are suggesting. You seem to be saying that I ended up feeling the way I did about Mordechai because of what his people had done to me and my family. In other words, the hardships I had suffered *caused* the feelings I came to have about Mordechai. Is that what you are suggesting?"

"It's what I'm wondering, anyway. Yes."

"And I'm proposing something entirely different," Yusuf responded. "I'm suggesting that my feelings about Mordechai were not caused by something others had done to me but by something I was doing to Mordechai. They were the result of a choice I was making relative to Mordechai. So," he continued, "how shall we evaluate these very different theories?" He looked around at the group.

"I don't know about evaluating them," Elizabeth said, "but Lou's theory leads to a pretty depressing outcome."

"Which is what?" Yusuf asked.

"That we're all just victims, powerless in the face of difficulty, inevitably doomed to be bitter and angry."

"I'm not saying that," Lou disagreed.

"I think you are," Elizabeth countered. "You said the only reason Yusuf wasn't bitter at the beginning of the story was because he simply wasn't thinking about his hardships for a moment. Remembering them caused him to feel bitter and angry again. If that doesn't make one powerless in the face of hardship, I don't know what does."

Lou had to admit she had a point. He didn't believe in that kind of helpless victimhood either. He knew of too many great souls who had passed through terrible mistreatment without becoming embittered by it to believe that mistreatment left us without choices. *But it does have an impact, doesn't it?* he wondered to himself, thinking of Cory.

"Excellent points, Elizabeth," Yusuf said. "I'd like to continue with your idea if I might."

"Certainly."

Yusuf looked around at the group. "Not having a memory at the forefront of my mind is different than having forgotten it. I can assure you that there has never been a moment in my life since my father's death that I haven't remembered that he died and how he died. Having said that, Lou is right that the level and nature of my focus is often very different from moment to moment. Lou reasoned that that fact allowed me to see Mordechai differently in the moment I had the inclination to help him. Actually, however, Lou's theory has it exactly backwards. It isn't that I saw Mordechai as a person because I wasn't dwelling on my hardships. Rather, it was that I wasn't dwelling on my hardships because I was seeing Mordechai as a person. I needed to dwell on my hardships only when I needed to be justified for treating Mordechai poorly. My hardships were my excuse at that point. When I didn't need an excuse, I was free not to dwell on them."

"Oh, so an abused woman is at fault for hating her abuser?" Gwyn mocked. "I'm sorry if I can't go there."

Yusuf paused and took in a deep breath. "I couldn't go there either, Gwyn," he said. "May I share a story with you?"

Gwyn didn't respond. Yusuf took a piece of paper out of a folder on a table in the front corner of the room. "This is from a letter I received in the mail a few years ago," he said. "It was written by one of our former students here who had fallen on very difficult times in her marriage. Rather than try to give you the context for it, I will let her speak for herself." He began reading.

One Friday more than a year ago, my estranged husband came to visit me at my parents' home. He came over relatively frequently, ostensibly to visit our daughter but really to try to win me back. Shortly before he left on this particular day, he asked me to show him a copy of our life insurance policy. He asked if we were paid up on it and asked me to double-check his reading of a phrase in the suicide clause. By the time I closed the door behind him that evening, his intentions were obvious. David was going to commit suicide. I said good-bye, expecting that I would never see my husband alive again.

I could hardly contain my excitement.

You see, my charming young groom had become violent shortly after our marriage. Within months, I had grown so terrified of him that I would not do anything, even turn on the television, without his approval. He was extremely jealous and soon forced me to throw away my address book, my high school yearbooks, and even pictures of my family. He threatened my life, humiliated me in public, flirted openly with other women, and finally reduced even our physical intimacy to violence.

All the while, he would occasionally show such amazing tenderness and remorse that for two years I could never bring myself to leave him. Finally, at the urging of our marriage counselor, I escaped to my parents' home. With their love and support, I slowly began to pull away from the bonds of my attachment to David. But he, more and more urgently, tried to win me back. I feared him, yet at the same time I needed him; I felt unable to free myself from the relationship. All in all, I was overjoyed to think that my nightmare might finally be ended with his suicide.

I was heartbroken when he appeared again the next morning. He was very depressed and proceeded to tell me the events of the night before. He admitted he had been planning to kill himself. He had gotten pills from a friend and had waited until nighttime so that nobody would be able to find him. Then he had sat down to compose his suicide note and will. After he had typed a few lines, the power suddenly went out. There wasn't even enough light for him to finish his note by hand. Without that sense of completion, he had been unable to go through with his plans. Then he told me that perhaps fate had interfered to keep him alive, and that this was a sign that he and I still belonged together.

As he told me this story, I felt fury. I had come so close to being rid of him, finally so close, and one tiny twist of fate had ruined it for me. I was still stuck with this cruel, unstable man, the man who had destroyed my confidence, who showed every intention of tormenting me the rest of my life. I had never before been so consumed with hate. My disappointment was so intense, I decided immediately what I would have to do. I knew, especially given his current emotional state, that if I handled the situation the right way he would likely try suicide again. So I opened my mouth to say, coldly, that I still thought he was a horrible monster and that I would never come back to him no matter what he did. I was about to say that I didn't care if he lived or died and that if anything, I preferred him dead. I was prepared to be as cruel as necessary to drive him back to suicide.

But then I paused. I still raged with hate, but I paused. I saw how close I was to encouraging a human being to die and was shocked by how far I was willing to carry my hate. I looked at him and was suddenly struck by something—something I learned at Camp Moriah. I was struck by his *personhood*, his humanity. Here before me was a person. A person with incredible emotional problems to be sure, but a person nonetheless. With his own deep hurts. His own heavy burdens. He himself had been raised in an abusive environment, with very little love and almost no kindness.

These thoughts made me cry. To my surprise, however, these were not tears of despair but tears of compassion. After all, this was a man who had intended to end his life. I found myself putting my arm around him to comfort him. It's a moment I still can't fully comprehend. In spite of everything he had done to me, I was consumed with love. And most surprising to me of all, from that moment—the moment I began seeing David as a person—I was never again tempted to return to the relationship. I had thought loving David meant I had to stay. That's partly why I had felt trapped. But it turned out in my case that being freed from the need for justification for not loving him is what allowed me to leave—and to do so compassionately and calmly, without the bitterness that could have burdened me for a lifetime.

Just as I learned at Camp Moriah, when I started seeing people, the world transformed around me. I now feel free— not just from an unhealthy relationship but from feelings that might otherwise have poisoned me. My life certainly would have been easier had I never married David. But I will always be glad I did not encourage him to die.

At that, Yusuf looked up from the letter. Clearing his throat, he said, "If someone is abused, my heart breaks for that person; what a cruel burden to have to carry. If I know such a person and he or she rages inside, should I be surprised? Of course not. Under such circumstances, I think to myself, *Who wouldn't?*

"In the face of that question, however, I find great hope in stories like the one I just read to you. For such stories show me that it is possible to find peace once more, even when much of my life has been a war zone.

"Although nothing I can do in the present can take away the mistreatment of the past, the way I carry myself in the present determines how I carry forward the memories of those mistreatments. When I see others as objects, I dwell on the injustices I have suffered in order to justify myself, keeping my mistreatments and suffering alive within me. When I see others as people, on the other hand, then I free myself from the need for justification. I therefore free myself from the need to focus unduly on the worst that has been done to me. I am free to leave the worst behind me, and to see not only the bad but the mixed and good in others as well.

"But none of that is possible," he continued, "if my heart is at war. A heart at war needs enemies to justify its warring. It needs enemies and mistreatment more than it wants peace."

"Yuck," Ria said under her breath.

"Yuck, indeed," Yusuf agreed. "Make no mistake. The outward wars around us started because of an inward war that went unnoticed: someone started seeing others as objects, and others used that as justification for doing the same. This is the germ, and germination, of war. When we're carrying this germ, we're just wars waiting to happen."

"What can you do about it?" Carol asked.

"To begin with," Yusuf responded, "we need to learn to look for the ways we're needing to be justified."

12 • Germs of Warfare

"Justification has some telltale signs," Yusuf began. "I've already mentioned a few—how we begin horribilizing others, for example. In fact, that sign is a subset of a whole category of signs that you might think of as exaggerations. When our hearts are at war, we tend to exaggerate others' faults; that's what we call horribilizing. We also tend to exaggerate the differences between ourselves and those we are blaming. We see little in common with them, when the reality is that we are similar in many if not most respects. We also exaggerate the importance of anything that will justify us. If I had had an appointment around the time Mordechai spilled his coins, for example, it would have suddenly seemed critical that I get to it. If I had happened to be carrying a book with me, I might have suddenly felt the need to bury my nose in it and start reading. Whenever we need to be justified, anything that will give us justification will immediately take on exaggerated importance in our life. Self-betrayal corrupts everything—even the value we place on things.

"And consider," he continued, "when in the Mordechai story did I start to devote my energy to blaming others? Before I betrayed myself or after?"

The group looked at the board. "After," Pettis answered first.

"And when in the story did I start feeling like a victim?"

"After you betrayed yourself," Ria said.

"And when in the story did I become consumed with the question of who's right and who's wrong? After I betrayed myself or before?"

"After."

"Are you noticing a pattern?" Yusuf asked. "I betrayed myself, and my whole world changed. It changed because I had chosen a different way of being in the world—a way that needed justification. Because I needed justification, I began to see everything in a self-justifying way. Others, myself, the world, my past, my present, my future, my hardships, my responsibilities, my view of everything became transformed—transformed for the purpose of feeling justified.

"As we betray ourselves over time, we develop characteristic styles of self-justification. One person, for example, might find justification in seeing himself as being better than others. If I think I am superior, I can excuse a lot of sins. Another might find justification in feeling he is entitled to things he isn't getting. After all, if others aren't giving me what they should, it isn't my fault if I blame them or treat them poorly. And so on.

"There are countless ways to feel justified, but I would like to introduce four common styles of justification. These are justification styles that all of us carry to one degree or another, but we might find that some of them are bigger for us than others. My hope is that pointing out these styles will help us to see ourselves a little more clearly and to discover some ways in which our own hearts are warring.

"The first of these is a style you'll immediately recognize from the Mordechai story. It's what we call the better-than style of justification, which is illustrated by the better-than box. This style of justification does not allow us to see others as people because we must see them prejudicially, as less than we are—less skilled perhaps, or less important, less knowledgeable, less righteous, and so on; but always less, and therefore always objects."

At that, Yusuf drew the following:

THE BETTER-THAN BOX

View of Myself Superior Important Virtuous/Right	**View of Others** Inferior Incapable/Irrelevant False/Wrong
Feelings Impatient Disdainful Indifferent	**View of World** Competitive Troubled Needs me

"I have a question," Pettis said, as Yusuf completed the quadrants of the box.

"Sure, go ahead."

"What if someone really is less talented at something, for example, and if I really am better in that area? Are you suggesting it's a self-justification simply to note that?"

"Not necessarily," Yusuf responded. "I can notice people's relative strengths and weaknesses when I'm seeing them as people. What's different when I'm in this box, however, is that I feel superior to or better than others because of these strengths or weaknesses. I use them to keep score of my and others' relative worth. So when I'm in this box, I'm doing more than simply noticing differences; I'm making judgments about peoples' worth based on those differences.

"Let me illustrate with a story. A few years ago, my wife, Lina, and I went out to a rather nice Mexican restaurant to celebrate Valentine's Day. When the attendant seated us, I immediately caught a whiff of the most repugnant smell of body odor imaginable. And it was coming from the next table! As I looked in that direction, I noticed the unkempt, slovenly person who was obviously the source. I was repulsed. *How dare he come out in public this way!* I raged within. *And on Valentine's Day of all days! He's going to ruin our evening!* In no time, this guy was an inconsiderate, filthy scumbag in my book."

"What a considerate man you were as well," Elizabeth murmured, a sly smile stealing across her face.

"I was just noticing another's deficiencies," Yusuf deadpanned.

"Quite," Elizabeth said, with knowing in her voice.

"Speaking of deficiencies," Yusuf continued, "Lina didn't seem too bothered by the smell. I'm not sure what bothered me more—the smell or Lina not being bothered by it. I began badgering her and complaining so much that Lina finally asked the waiter to seat us elsewhere. Thankfully, from our new location in the next section of the restaurant I could only faintly smell the man's stench.

"When our food came, however, the body odor stench came with it! *Did the waiter stink too?* I wondered. He looked clean enough, so I looked around to see if the smelly man had just walked near us. But he was still seated across the way at his table. Then I noticed that the stench was coming from my plate of food! It turns out that this restaurant's black beans had a peculiar smell to them—a smell I had mistaken as body odor."

"Who would have thought—scumbag beans," Elizabeth joked.

"Right," Yusuf laughed.

"That's a nice story, turning out as it did," Gwyn said. "But what if the man really did stink? What if you weren't mistaken?"

"That's exactly the question I want to ask as well, Gwyn," Yusuf agreed. "What about that?" he asked the group. "What if I was right?"

"I have a thought about that," Elizabeth spoke up, "as I've been in this kind of box ever since we began this morning."

"Really," Yusuf said. "How so?"

"I have been upset at my sister for not making the effort to be here for her boy. Someone had to come, so I came for her. That's a dangerous combination of facts for someone who is prone to feeling superior, isn't it?" she said, blowing her hair out of her eyes in mock exasperation. "I've been sitting here thinking about this while you've been talking, and here's what's occurred to me: I still think she should have made the effort to come. I think I am right about that. But I haven't been able to stop at simply noticing the problem. I've come to obsess over it. I'm wallowing in unproductive thoughts and feelings as much as you, Yusuf, were wallowing in smelly vapors."

"Yes," Yusuf chuckled. "You're suggesting that even if I am right about something, my emotional experience will be entirely different in the box than it would be if I were out."

"Well, yes, I'm wondering," she said. "Just like you've written there in the feelings area of the box, I've been impatient about being here, and I'm filled with disdain for my sister and her husband for not earning more, not making this the financial priority they should. I'm filled with how they are a problem family, how my sister has always made poor choices in my eyes, how they fail their children, and so on."

Elizabeth paused, her mind many miles away with her family. "I think I have made myself into an insufferable know-it-all," she muttered, while looking vacantly across the room.

"If so," Yusuf said, "you'll have that in common with a lot of us. I certainly justified myself in this way toward Mordechai, for example, didn't I?"

Most in the room nodded, but Elizabeth was still lost in thought.

"Let's consider a second common style of justification, shall we?" he said, as he walked to the board. "It's a style we call the I-deserve box."

"By the way," he added, as he began to write, "people who go around feeling better-than generally feel entitled to a lot of things, so these two styles of justification often come together."

THE I-DESERVE BOX

View of Myself	View of Others
Meritorious	Mistaken
Mistreated/Victim	Mistreating
Unappreciated	Ungrateful
Feelings	**View of World**
Entitled	Unfair
Deprived	Unjust
Resentful	Owes me

As Yusuf finished writing, he said, "When I'm in this kind of box, I typically feel mistreated, victimized, entitled, deprived, resentful, and so on. Did I have any of these thoughts and feelings in the Mordechai story?"

"Yes," the group answered.

"I believe you're right," Yusuf agreed. "If I had been alive to how such thoughts and feelings are designed to give me justification, I might have been able to recognize that something was crooked in how I was being. I might have been able to find my way back to seeing Mordechai merely as he was, as a person.

"But I didn't recognize my crookedness, of course, and I went on viewing Mordechai more or less as an object for many years. And most of the other Mordechais I met as well," he added. "Which is to say that I was feeling justified in both the better-than and I-deserve ways in the Mordechai story, and probably in the black beans story too. When I'm seeing others crookedly, what I need in that moment is justification, and I'll find it any way I can get it—whether by seeing myself as better, as entitled, both, and so on.

"Before we leave the black beans story," Yusuf continued, "I want to address two additional points: First of all, notice how my better-than and I-deserve boxes set me up to be mistaken about this man. When would I be more likely to mistake the source of the offensive odor—when I look disdainfully and resentfully at others or when I simply see people?"

"When you look disdainfully and resentfully at them, no question," Pettis answered.

"So notice," Yusuf continued, "the more sure I am that I'm right, the more likely I will actually be mistaken. My need to be right makes it more likely that I will be wrong! Likewise, the more sure I am that I am mistreated, the more likely I am to miss ways that I am mistreating others myself. My need for justification obscures the truth."

"Interesting," Pettis said, while turning the ideas over in his mind. The others appeared to be working hard on them as well.

"Yes," Yusuf agreed. "One more point about the story before we move on. In order to make it, I'm going to change the scenario slightly. Let's say this story happened at home or in the workplace. Let's also assume, as Gwyn raised earlier, that this person really did have a body odor problem. In that case, which version of me—the better-than, the I-deserve, or the seeing-person version—do you suppose would be more likely to be able to help him overcome his problem?"

"Oh, I'd imagine that the seeing-person version would be more helpful," Pettis answered.

"Why?"

"Well," Pettis hesitated, "if you went to him when you were thinking he was a filthy lowlife or when you felt he owed you something, you'd probably invite him to resist you."

"Does everyone agree with that?" Yusuf asked.

"I'm not sure that I do," Lou said. "I'm worried that if you just saw him as a person, you might not talk to him at all. You might just let it slide."

Yusuf smiled. "You're still worried that seeing others as people means you have to be soft, aren't you, Lou?"

"Maybe I am, maybe I'm not," Lou smiled coyly. "It just seems like you might let this kind of thing slide rather than hurt someone's feelings. That's all I'm saying."

"Would I be likely to just let it slide if I really cared about the man?" Yusuf responded. "Would I just let him stink and therefore let everyone think poorly of him? Is that what someone who really cares about another is likely to do?"

"Well, no, I suppose not," Lou allowed.

"In fact," Yusuf continued, "when I let people go on hurting themselves and others without making the effort to help them to change, it is rarely because I am seeing them as a person. Usually it's because I am being motivated by yet another kind of self-justification, a justification that very often causes people to go soft and to feel justified by their softness."

"That is something I would be interested in hearing about," Lou said.

"I thought you might," Yusuf smiled.

13 · *More Germ Warfare*

"In fact," Yusuf replied, "Avi will tell you that his most common justification style invites him to go soft."

The group looked over at Avi.

"True," Avi nodded. "Shall I share some thoughts about it?" he asked Yusuf.

"Please."

"When we find justification in softness," Avi began, "it's usually because we're carrying around a third basic kind of justification box, a box we call the must-be-seen-as box.

"It looks something like this:"

THE MUST-BE-SEEN-AS BOX

View of Myself	View of Others
Need to be well thought of	Judgmental
Fake	Threatening
	My audience

Feelings	View of World
Anxious/Afraid	Dangerous
Needy/Stressed	Watching
Overwhelmed	Judging me

"When I'm carrying around this kind of justification box," Avi said, as he finished up the diagram, "I might be worried about being seen as likable, for example. Such a box will keep me from being able to do the helpful and right thing when the helpful or right thing might be something the other person won't like. Let me give you an example of that.

"Early on in our time here at Camp Moriah," he began, "I hired a man named Jack as our field director—the person who runs everything out on the trail with the youth. It didn't take me too long to discover I had made a mistake. It turned out that Jack was a very poor manager of people. He had an ill temper and always blamed problems on others. He carried a better-than box that made out everyone he worked with to be inferior. As a result, he dismissed criticism out of hand, blamed every failure on others, and generally treated his coworkers with indifference and disdain. He was creating problems everywhere. I saw what was going on, of course, and knew that if he was ever going to make it here, he simply would have to change the way he worked and the way he managed. But you know what? I never said anything to him about it. He had a pretty volatile personality, and I was afraid to confront him with the problem. So I didn't. Instead, I just started hoping he would move or decide to take another job!"

"That's what I'm talking about," Lou blurted. "That's exactly what has me worried about what you're saying here—that it will make people paralyzingly soft."

"But was I seeing Jack as a person in this story, Lou?"

Lou thought for a second. He wanted to say yes, but he suddenly began to see Yusuf and Avi's point.

"If he'd have been a person to me, then I would have cared enough about him to want to help him succeed, don't you think?" Avi said.

Lou didn't say anything. He saw that he was on the losing side of this one.

"I agree, Lou, that my softness here as a manager was a problem, but I would suggest that in this case I was soft precisely because I saw Jack as an object, not because I saw him as a person. I had a must-be-seen-as box about being likable, or perhaps about not having problems, which caused me to completely ignore what would have been most helpful to Jack and to Camp Moriah. As Yusuf mentioned a moment ago, this kind of justification box—the must-be-seen-as variety—often invites us to go soft."

Despite himself, Lou nodded ever so slightly.

"This is also the kind of justification," Yusuf jumped in, "that Pettis noticed in the Mordechai story when he reasoned that my turning away might have been motivated by a desire not to appear wantonly callous. In other words, I was making a presentation of myself; I had a need for others to see me in a way that justified me. It is similarly the kind of justification box that was behind me pushing the lettuce under the counter, where no one could reasonably argue that I should have seen it and therefore have picked it up. My pushing the lettuce away shows that I had a need to be seen perhaps as considerate or responsible or tidy—qualities others would not ascribe to me if they thought I consciously left the lettuce there. Of course, the fact that I didn't just bend over and pick it up, which couldn't have taken any more energy than scooting it away, suggests that I might also have been carrying around one of the earlier justification boxes we discussed. Which one, would you say?"

"You're too important to pick up lettuce," Gwyn answered. "It sounds to me like you have a better-than box."

"Yes, Gwyn, excellent," Yusuf agreed. "I think that's right. "Which means, put another way, that I saw Lina as just unimportant enough that she should be the one to have to worry about that kind of thing."

He paused to let that settle.

"How would it be to live with someone who thought of you like that?"

This comment thrust Lou into the middle of a problem that had barely occurred to him until this moment. He hadn't bent over to pick up the lettuce pieces or their equivalents in his home for years, if ever. Unlike Yusuf, he never bothered to hide the evidence either. It didn't matter to him that it fell on the floor; he couldn't be bothered by such trivialities. But now Yusuf's words rang in his head: *I saw Lina as just unimportant enough that she should be the one to have to worry about that kind of thing. How would it be to live with someone who thought of you like that?*

In this moment, Lou knew that Carol could answer that question. And he knew that she was probably sitting there thinking that very thing. With this thought, Lou suddenly noticed a sensation that was almost completely foreign to him, it had been so long since he had last felt it: he started to feel a prickly heat, as if someone had suddenly turned up the thermostat. And then he felt his ears go red and his cheeks flush. And then he knew— he was embarrassed! And then he felt embarrassed that he was embarrassed and felt his face flush all the hotter.

He looked at the diagram of the better-than box—superior, important, virtuous, right, impatient, disdainful, indifferent; others are inferior, incapable, wrong, and so on.

He felt nailed.

And then his mind reeled back to a conversation he had had with Cory on the plane: "I suppose you think I've really done you wrong, Dad." Cory had said. "You're even upset to be on this plane. You think it's just another waste of time I've caused you."

Cory was right. Lou was angry about having to be on that plane, having to spend this time away when his company was coming unglued. All because of a son who lacked even a shred of gratitude for everything Lou had offered him, a son who was ruining the family name. *It isn't fair that one boy could ruin so much!* Lou shouted within.

The word "unfair" suddenly leaped from his thoughts, and he looked up at the board once more: The I-deserve box—you see life as unfair and others as ungrateful and mistreating. You are prone to resentment and to feelings of entitlement.

It's true, Lou thought to himself. *He did feel like he deserved a better son—like his older son, Jesse.* And then Yusuf's words rang in his mind again: *"How would it be to live with someone who thought of you like that?"*

Lou shook his head and looked again at the diagrams: the must-be-seen-as box—need to be thought well of. *No, I couldn't give a damn,* Lou thought. *I don't have that one.* But then he noticed that this style of self-justification often sees others as threatening. And he knew in that moment that he did see Cory that way. Cory threatened the family reputation and name. He put Lou's reputation at risk. *I'll be damned,* Lou thought in surprise, *I do care what others think of me.*

"Finally," came Avi's voice, pulling Lou back into the present, "there is a fourth common category of self-justification. It came up in our Mordechai discussion when one of you mentioned that Yusuf might have become depressed by the thought that he was actually a bad person. This style is illustrated by the worse-than box. He then drew the following:

THE WORSE-THAN BOX

View of Myself	View of Others
Not as good	Advantaged
Broken/Deficient	Privileged
Fated	Blessed
Feelings	**View of World**
Helpless	Hard/Difficult
Jealous/Bitter	Against me
Depressed	Ignoring me

"Can I ask a question about this one?" Carol said.

"Of course, Carol, anything."

"I've been wondering about this kind of view since the Mordechai story," she continued. "Frankly, I see a lot of myself in this one, but I don't see how I feel justified when I'm seeing things in this way. In fact, if anything, I feel just the opposite. For example, when I was in the middle of my eating disorder, I just felt worthless and no good. I didn't feel justified at all."

Avi nodded. "Let me share something with you," he said.

"I had a speech impediment until I was nearly twenty. I stuttered terribly. I can't tell you how embarrassing it was. I pulled away from others and looked for every excuse to be alone. Did I know I had a problem? Yes. And it was my problem, I knew that. But it affected my view of others. I looked at them longingly, not out of any kind of love or concern, but rather out of a kind of nagging jealousy. I was jealous that I couldn't be more like them, jealous of how easily speech came to them. I was always afraid I would encounter a block, that my eyelids would flutter pathetically while I tried to spit out the words. I imagined this scene many times, and I lived in perpetual fear of looking ridiculous.

"So did I feel justified?" he continued. "It depends what you mean by that. I wasn't justifying my stuttering, since stuttering itself doesn't need justification. There is no crookedness toward others in merely having trouble with speech, or in any other disability for that matter. While I wasn't justifying my disability, however, I was justifying something else. In fact, I was actually using my disability to justify something else—something that *was* crooked, something that required justification. I used my disability as justification for separating myself from others. This— the separation from others as people—is what needed justifying, for it was this act that was crooked. I turned from people at every opportunity, not allowing myself to be penetrated by their needs, and blamed my disability all the while. I told myself that I couldn't be expected to do this thing and that given my disability. My disability was my justification! It was my excuse for failing to engage with the world."

At this, Carol started nodding. "Okay, I think I get it then," she said. "So in my case, it may not be that I was feeling justified for my eating disorder but that I might have started to use my disorder as an excuse for why I couldn't be better with others."

"That is worth thinking about," Avi said. He then gazed back at the boxes he and Yusuf had written on the board. "As I look at these boxes," he said, "and compare my early life against them, I would say that I can certainly relate to the worse-than box. I would say that I can relate as well to the must-be-seen-as box. In fact, in my life the must-be-seen-as and worse-than justifications have often come together. While suffering from my stuttering, I desperately wanted others to think well of me. As a result, I almost never spoke because I was afraid that I would look foolish. Just as that box suggests, I viewed others as judgmental and threatening, and I always felt as if I was being watched, listened to, and evaluated. Cutting myself off from others as people, I lived in perpetual fear and anxiety. And the more I cut myself off from them, the more the anxiety grew."

Carol pondered this. "Yes, I can see that in myself as well," she said. "I think I sometimes pull away and try to just slink off into the shadows. Lou here is such a successful and accomplished person, a lot of times I don't think that I measure up, and I end up getting really down on myself."

Avi nodded. "I know the feeling. I spent most of my first twenty years feeling the same way."

"What did you do about it?" Carol asked. "Was it just as simple as getting rid of your stutter?"

Avi smiled. "Believe me, getting rid of the stutter wasn't easy at all."

"No, that's not what I meant," Carol said, turning pink.

"I know, I know, don't worry about it," he said. "I'm just teasing. But in answer to your question, Carol, stuttering wasn't the problem."

At that, Avi looked down at the floor for a moment. "How do I know?" he continued, looking back up at the group. "Because I tried to commit suicide twice after I had mostly overcome my stuttering."

This mention seemed almost to suck the air out of the room. It was as though everyone stopped breathing for a moment, their minds too interested in what Avi had just said to bother with the mundane details of moment-to-moment living.

"One time with pills, one time with a razor blade," he said, as he squinted in recollection. "The second time around, my mother found me on the bathroom floor in a pool of blood."

14 · *The Path to War*

Avi yanked himself from the memory of his suicide attempts and looked squarely at Carol.

"So no, Carol," he said, "my stuttering was not the cause of my problems. Rather, I carried a heart at war—a heart at war with others, myself, and the world. I had been using my stuttering as a weapon in that war and had gotten myself into a place where I was seeing and feeling crookedly and self-justifyingly. *That* was my problem. And I wasn't able to find my way out of it until I found my way out of my need for justification."

"How were you able to do it?" Carol asked, her voice barely more than a whisper. "How did you get rid of your need for justification?"

Avi smiled at her. "That, Carol, will be our topic for tomorrow."

"You're going to leave it at that?" Lou asked Avi. "You just told us you tried to commit suicide twice and now we're just going to leave for the evening?"

Avi chuckled. "You want to hear more about it?"

"Well, I don't know," Lou pulled back. "Maybe."

"I'll tell you more about it tomorrow," Avi promised. "But in our last forty minutes or so this evening, I think it would be best to review what we've covered today. That way, we'll come back tomorrow with a solid understanding.

"First of all," he began, "we've talked about two ways of being: one with the heart at war, where we see others as objects, and the other with the heart at peace, where we see others as people. And you'll remember that we learned that we can do almost any behavior, whether hard, soft, or in between, in either of these ways. Here are two questions for you then: If we can do almost any outward behavior with our hearts either at peace or at war, why should we care which way we are being? Does it matter?"

"Yes," Carol answered. "It definitely matters."

"Why?" Avi asked. "Why do you think it matters?"

"Because I've seen how a heart at war ruins everything."

Avi waited for more.

Carol continued. "I've been acting outwardly nice toward our boy Cory ever since he started getting into trouble, but I've known that I didn't really mean it. And this has done a couple of things to me. First of all, I think I have played into an I-deserve box that has me thinking I am being nothing but sweet and kind, and he's just mistreating me and the rest of the family. And Cory can tell that's how I'm feeling. I know because he's called me on it many times. Although I always deny his accusations," she added meekly.

"I think I've also spent most of the last few years feeling a gnawing guilt knowing that I'm not really loving Cory, even though I've been making it look like I do." She paused for a moment. In the silence that followed, her eyes suddenly began filling with tears. A single drop cascaded over her lid and streamed down her cheek. "And no good mother does that," she choked, as she wiped the moisture away. She began to shake her head. "No good mother does that." She paused again for a moment. "I think I've developed a worse-than box—that I'm a bad mom."

"I think you're being too hard on yourself," Lou said. "The truth is Cory has been a terribly difficult boy. It's not your fault."

"It depends what you mean by that, Lou," she said, regaining her composure. "I understand that I may not be responsible for the things he's done. But I am responsible for what I've done."

"Yes, but you've done nothing but good," Lou offered. "I'm the one who's been the jerk with him."

"But Lou, don't you see? We're talking about something deeper than merely what I've done or haven't done. Yes, I've cooked his meals and cleaned his clothes. I've stood there and taken his abusive language, and more. But that's just on the surface. The point is that while I've been playing the part of the outward pacifist, my heart has been swinging at him. *And* at you," she added, "for the way you outwardly war with him. I've been at war too, but just in a way that makes it seem like I'm not."

"But who wouldn't be, under the circumstances?" Lou countered. "At war, that is."

"But that can't be the answer, Lou! It can't."

"Why not?"

"Because then we're all doomed. That's to say that our entire experience, even our thoughts and feelings, are controlled and caused by others. It's to believe that we're not responsible for who we've become."

"But damn it, Carol, don't you see what Cory is doing? He's making you feel guilty for stuff he's doing. What about Cory being responsible?"

"But in the world you describe, Lou, he couldn't be responsible. If we can't be expected to react to a heart that's at war with anything but warring hearts ourselves, how can we expect or demand that he act any differently to us, when our hearts too are warring?"

"But he caused it all!" Lou bellowed. "We've always given him everything he's needed! It's his fault! You're about to let him off the hook and take it all upon yourself. I won't allow it!"

Carol took in a deep breath and exhaled heavily, her body shuddering with deep hurt as she did so. She looked at her lap and then closed her eyes, her face drawn in pain.

"What are you afraid of, Lou?" Yusuf spoke up.

"Afraid? I'm not afraid of anything," Lou said.

"Then what is it you feel you cannot allow?"

"I can't allow my boy to get away with destroying my family!"

Yusuf nodded. "You're right, Lou. You can't."

That was not the answer Lou had been expecting.

"But that is not what Carol is suggesting. She hasn't said anything about letting Cory off the hook. She's only been talking about not letting herself off the hook."

"No, she's sitting here blaming herself for things that are Cory's fault."

"Like what? Has she said that the drugs and the stealing were her fault?"

"No, but she's saying that she's been a bad mother, when the fact of the matter is that any halfway good son wouldn't have ever made her feel that way."

"And Cory didn't, that's her point," Yusuf said.

"Didn't what?"

"Didn't make her feel that way."

"Yes he did!"

"That's not what I heard *her* say."

Lou turned to Carol. "Look, Carol," he began, "I know you're upset, but I don't want you to take on more than you are able. I don't want you to internalize problems that aren't yours, that's all."

Carol smiled at Lou, her face painted in melancholy. "I know, Lou. Thank you. But Yusuf's right."

"Right about what?"

"That I am responsible for how I have been feeling, not only for what I have been doing."

"But you wouldn't have been feeling that way if it wasn't for Cory!"

She nodded. "You may be right."

"See!" Lou pounced. "That's what I mean."

"Yes, I think I do see, Lou, but I'm afraid that you still do not."

"What do you mean?"

"The fact that I wouldn't have felt the way I've come to feel if it weren't for Cory doesn't mean he has caused me to feel as I have."

"On the contrary, of course that's what it means," Lou objected.

"No, Lou, it doesn't. And here's how I know: I'm not feeling that way now. Cory has done everything he has done—everything he has done in the past, everything I have blamed for how I have been feeling—but I don't feel the same now. Which means that he hasn't caused me to feel how I've felt. I've always had the choice."

"But he makes the choice difficult!" Lou objected.

"Yes," Yusuf stepped in. "He likely does, Lou. But difficult choices are still choices. No one, whatever their actions, can deprive me of the ability to choose my own way of being. Difficult people are nevertheless people, and it always remains in my power to see them that way."

"And then get eaten up by them," Lou muttered.

"That's not what he's saying, Lou!" Carol pleaded. "Seeing someone as a person doesn't mean you have to be soft. The Saladin story showed us that. Even war is possible with a heart at peace. But you know that, Lou. You've been here the whole time I have, and you're a smart man. Which means that if these are really still questions for you, then you are refusing to hear.

Why, Lou? Why are you refusing to hear?"

This rebuke caught Lou short. Normally, he would have pounced all over such a pointed comment and leveled the insufferable soul who had made it. But he had no such urge in the moment. Carol, ever meek, even timid, had perhaps never criticized him so directly. Certainly never in front of others. And yet here she was, countering Lou's complaint that she was letting others off the hook by refusing to let Lou off the hook! Lou began to marvel that he was learning lessons on outward toughness from the most gentle person he knew. He had worried that this course would invite people to be weak and soft, and yet Carol seemed to be metamorphosing in the other direction right before his eyes. *"Some justification boxes make people go soft,"* Lou remembered. *Maybe Carol has had those kind of boxes,* Lou thought. *And so maybe getting out of the box for her will invite her to be more forceful at times.*

But that's not my problem, he chuckled. *If I'm in these boxes, they must be boxes that invite me to go hard—really hard, in fact.* He chuckled again. *So maybe getting out of them will mean that I will soften up some.*

Despite the epiphanies, that thought worried Lou.

"Lou," came Yusuf's voice, ripping him away from his thoughts. "Are you okay?"

"Yes, fine. I'm fine."

He leaned over to Carol. "I think I may be recovering a bit of my hearing," he whispered.

I'll be damned, he thought, *I am going soft.* But suddenly he wasn't so worried about it.

"So—" Yusuf continued, looking around at the group. "In response to Avi's question, Carol has suggested that the issue deeper than our behavior—our way of being—matters. A lot. Do you agree?"

Lou nodded along with the others.

"Then I have another question for you. If the choice of way of being is important, then how do we change from one way to the other? Specifically, how do we change from peace to war—from seeing people to seeing objects?"

"Through self-betrayal," Elizabeth answered.

"Which is what?" Yusuf asked.

"It's what you illustrated through the Mordechai story. You had a sense to help him, which means you were seeing him as a person, but then you turned away, and began to justify why you shouldn't have to help him, and he became an object to you."

"Yes, excellent, Elizabeth," Yusuf said. "That is exactly right. So self-betrayal—this act of violating my own sensibilities toward another person—causes me to see that person or persons differently, and not only them but myself and the world also. When I have the impression to help my spouse clean the kitchen, for example, but stay planted on the couch instead, I begin to see her and myself in ways that justify my failure to help. For example, I might begin seeing her as too demanding and myself as deserving a break. When I ignore the sense to apologize to my son, I might start telling myself that he's really the one who needs to apologize, or that he's a pain in the backside, or that if I apologize, he'll just take it as license to do what he wants. And so on.

"Which is to say," he continued, "that when I violate the sensibility I have about others and how I should be toward them, I immediately begin to see the world in ways that justify my self-betrayal. In those moments, I am beginning to see and live crookedly, which creates the need within me to be justified."

"But what if I don't have those impressions to help to begin with?" Lou asked. "I actually don't think I have them very often, to tell you the truth. Does that mean I'm not betraying myself?"

"It might," Yusuf allowed. "But it could also mean something else."

"What?"

Yusuf pointed at the choice diagram.

THE CHOICE DIAGRAM

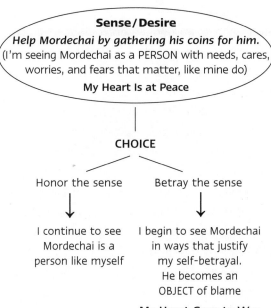

Sense/Desire

Help Mordechai by gathering his coins for him.
(I'm seeing Mordechai as a PERSON with needs, cares, worries, and fears that matter, like mine do)

My Heart Is at Peace

CHOICE

Honor the sense   Betray the sense

I continue to see
Mordechai is a
person like myself

I begin to see Mordechai
in ways that justify
my self-betrayal.
He becomes an
OBJECT of blame

My Heart Goes to War

View of Myself	View of Mordechai
Better than	No right to be there
A victim (so owed)	Robs me of peace
Bad (but made to be)	Zionist threat
Want to be seen well	Bigot
Feelings	**View of World**
Angry	Unfair
Depressed	Unjust
Bitter	Burdensome
Justified	Against me

"What do you suppose happens," he said, "if I get in this box here toward Mordechai and then don't get out?"

No one responded for a moment.

"Nothing will happen," Lou finally said. "Everything will stay the same."

"Yes, Lou, which is to say that I will end up carrying that box with me, right?"

"Yes, I guess that's right," Lou responded slowly, trying to grasp the implications.

At that, Yusuf added an arrow to the diagram, signifying how the box can travel with us.

"In other words," Yusuf resumed, "If I get in this box and don't get out, I end up taking the box with me. And in my next interaction with Mordechai, I am likely to start in the box— from the very beginning, right?"

Yusuf waited to see comprehension in the eyes before him. Sensing that they were understanding, he continued. "And if I'm already starting in the box, do you suppose I would be likely to have a sense or desire to help in my next interaction with Mordechai or with others I lump together with him?"

"Oh, I see," Lou said. "No, you wouldn't. You would start out bothered and bitter and angry. And in that state you probably wouldn't have a sense to help at all."

"That's what I'm suggesting," Yusuf agreed. "I can end up living in a big box from which I already perceive people as objects. When I develop such bigger boxes, I erupt whenever my justifications in the box are challenged or threatened. If I need to be seen as smart, for example, I will get anxious whenever I think my intelligence might be at issue—as, for example, when I am asked to speak in public or when I believe others are evaluating me. If I feel superior, I will be likely to erupt in anger or disdain if others fail to recognize how I am better, or if I perceive that someone is trying to make himself look better than me. And so on. I no longer need to betray my sense regarding another in order to be in the box toward him because I am already in the box. I am always on the lookout for offense when I'm in the box, and I will erupt whenever my justification claims are threatened."

"So you're saying that if I find I don't have many such senses, it may be an indication that I'm already in a box, that I'm carrying my boxes with me, so to speak."

"I'm suggesting that possibility, yes."

Lou pondered this.

"I have a different question from Lou's," Carol said, raising her hand.

"Sure, go ahead."

"My problem isn't that I have too few of these senses to help. I'm worried that I have too many. And frankly, as I think about this, I'm a bit overwhelmed that I have to do everything I feel I should do in order not to betray myself."

"I have the same question," Ria said.

Yusuf nodded. "It's a good thing, then, that that's not what this means."

"It's not?" Carol asked hopefully.

"No. And to see why not, let's look at the choice diagram again. Notice two elements of the diagram: First, notice that we use the words 'honor' and 'betray' rather than 'do' or 'not do.' Notice as well the word 'desire' along with 'sense.' In other words, this sense we're describing is something akin to a desire. You with me?" he asked Carol before continuing.

"Yes. 'Honor' and 'betray,' and 'desire'—I see them."

"Okay, then, let me ask you this: Have you ever been in a situation where you ultimately weren't able to do something you felt you should do for somebody, but nevertheless still wished that you could have done it?"

"Sure, all the time," Carol answered. "That's exactly what I'm talking about."

Yusuf nodded in acknowledgment. "Notice how those experiences are different from this experience of mine. In my case, after I failed to help, did I still have a desire to help?"

Carol looked at the diagram. "No."

"No, I didn't. You're exactly right. So notice the difference: in my case, I started with a desire to help but ended with contempt, whereas in your case, you started with a desire to help and ended with a desire to help."

He paused to let that sink in.

"Although it may be true in such cases that you didn't perform the outward service you felt would have been ideal, you still retained the sense or desire you had in the beginning. That is, you still *desired* to be helpful. My guess is that there were probably a number of other things that needed to happen, and you just couldn't do this additional ideal thing. Am I right?"

Carol nodded.

"And that's life," Yusuf shrugged. "We quite commonly have many things that would be ideal to do at any given moment. Whether or not we perform a particular service, the way we can know if we've betrayed ourselves is by whether we are still desiring to be helpful."

"Okay, I think I get it," Carol said. "So you're saying that the sense I'm either honoring or not is this desire of helpfulness, not the mere fact of doing or not doing any particular behavior."

"Yes, Carol, that's exactly what I'm saying. And that's why we use 'honor' and 'betray' on the choice diagram rather than 'do' or 'not do.'

"Incidentally," he continued, "this shows how I can actually behave the way I feel would be ideal but nevertheless still be in the box. Think about the Mordechai story. Let's say that after I got in the box, I saw someone who knew me, and then out of shame, not wanting to appear insensitive, I turned and helped Mordechai gather his coins, all the while fuming that I was being made to do it. In that case, was I seeing him as a person while I was helping?"

"No."

"Had I retained my desire of helpfulness?"

"No, you hadn't."

"So had I honored or betrayed my sense of helpfulness?"

"You'd betrayed it," Carol said. "Okay, I get it. It's not simply about the behavior, is it? It's deeper than that."

"Exactly. My heart wasn't at peace even though I was being outwardly helpful, which suggests that I had betrayed my original desire to help."

Carol winced at that comment and bit her lip. "Then that raises another question for me."

"Go ahead."

"The situation you described—retaining my desire to help even when I can't help—explains some of my experiences, but not all of them."

"Go on," Yusuf invited.

"Well, a lot of times, when I can't help, I don't think I feel peaceful anymore either. To be quite honest, sometimes I'm burning up inside. I feel overwhelmed—all anxious and stressed because I can't help. It eats me up, and I can't seem to relax or find peace. Like when my house isn't clean, for example. I get anxious when we have others over if I haven't been able to clean up."

"Ah," Yusuf responded, "then in those cases it sounds like you might be in the box, doesn't it?"

Carol nodded.

"And you might, Carol. Ultimately, you're the only person who would know for sure, but it sounds like you might have developed a hyperactive must-be-seen-as box. Maybe you have a box about needing to be seen as helpful, for example, or thoughtful or kind or as a kind of superwoman. Any must-be-seen-as boxes like those would likely multiply in your mind the list of obligations you think you have to meet and would likely rob you of peace when you aren't able to meet them."

Carol slumped slightly in her chair. "That's me to a T," she said. "That's exactly what I'm like."

She looked up at Yusuf. "Then where do they come from?"

"Where do *what* come from?"

"These boxes—like this must-be-seen-as box."

"Again, let's look at the choice diagram," he said.

Pointing at it, he continued, "When in that story did I have a box—whether of the better-than, I-deserve, worse-than, or must-be-seen-as varieties?"

"After you betrayed your sense."

"Exactly. Which is to say that we construct our boxes through a lifetime of choices. Every time we choose to pull away from and blame another, we necessarily feel justified in doing so, and we start to plaster together a box of self-justification, the walls getting thicker and thicker over time."

"But why have I developed a must-be-seen-as box as opposed to some of the others?" Carol followed up.

"Good question, Carol," Yusuf said. "If you're like most people, you've probably developed boxes that have elements from each of these styles of justification."

"I think I'm usually in the worse-than or must-be-seen-as categories," Carol said.

"Not me," Lou interjected, "better-than and I-deserve all the way."

"What a surprise," Gwyn joked.

"Yes, shocking," Elizabeth agreed.

"I wouldn't want to disappoint you," Lou said. "You're expecting it of me now."

"So why do Lou and I have different kinds of boxes?" Carol asked, returning to the question at hand.

"With respect to the box," Yusuf responded, "don't be too taken in by the categories. They are simply linguistic tools that help us think a little more precisely about the issue of justification. The differences they show are in key ways artificial. What I mean is that our similarities are much greater than our differences. What you and Lou share with everyone else on the planet is a need to be justified that has arisen through a lifetime of self-betrayals. If we justify ourselves in different ways, it is because we justify ourselves within a context, and we will reach for the easiest justification we can find. So, for example, if I had been raised in a critical or demanding environment, it might have been easier for me, relatively speaking, to find refuge in worse-than or must-be-seen-as justifications. Those who were raised in affluent or sanctimonious environments, on the other hand, may naturally gravitate to better-than and I-deserve justifications, and so on. Must-be-seen-as boxes might easily arise in such circumstances as well.

"But the key point, and the point that is the same for all of us, is that we all grab for justification, however we can get it. Because grabbing for justification is something we do, we can undo it. Whether we find justification in how we are worse or in how we are better, we can each find our way to a place where we have no need for justification at all. We can find our way to peace—deep, lasting, authentic peace—even when war is breaking out around us."

"How?" Carol asked.

"As Avi said a few minutes ago, that is our topic for tomorrow.

"For tonight, we invite you to ponder what boxes you are carrying, and the nature of your predominant self-justifications.

"I also invite you to consider how your box—this warring heart that you carry within—has invited outward war between you and those in your life.

Remember this collusion diagram?" he asked, pointing at the picture of Avi and Hannah's conflict about the edging.

Most of the group nodded.

"Look for that pattern in your own lives tonight," he said. "See where you might be inviting in others the very behavior you are complaining about. Ponder what boxes might be behind your reactions in those situations. Try to figure out what self-justifications you are defending."

Yusuf looked around at the group. "In short, our invitation to you for tonight," he said, "is to notice your battles and to ponder your wars. Using the conflict in the Middle East metaphorically, we are, all of us, Palestinian and Israeli in some areas of our lives. It will serve neither ourselves nor our loved ones to think that we are better.

"Have a good evening."

PART III

From War to Peace

15 · *Apologies*

Lou barely slept that night. He tossed and turned as the mistakes of the last thirty years or so played themselves over and over in his mind. Cory was an object to him, he couldn't deny it. His heart stirred in anger merely at the thought of Cory's name. But there was a new feeling this night—a desire to be rid of the ache he felt regarding Cory rather than a desire to be rid of Cory himself. He was wanting his son back. Or perhaps more accurately, he was beginning to feel the desire to be Cory's father again.

Speaking of ache, the pain he felt for banishing Kate was now acute. As he replayed what he had regarded as the mutinous meeting in the boardroom, he heard his words and witnessed his scowl afresh. He had been a child! He couldn't afford to lose Kate, but his pride had driven him over a cliff and blinded him to a truth he suspected was obvious to everyone else—that Kate, not Lou, was the prime mover behind Zagrum Company's success. *How could I have been so blind! What am I going to do? How can I rescue the company?*

But by the wee hours of the morning, his thoughts and pain were located elsewhere. For thirty-one years, Carol (who, he noted, had slept soundly through the night) had given her life to him, while he had given too little in return. They met at a dance at Syracuse University. Carol was on a date with one of Lou's friends. Lou, alone that night, couldn't take his eyes off her. He began the evening wondering whether it would be ethical to move in on his friend. By the end of the evening, it was no longer a matter of ethics, only of strategy.

Over the months that followed, Lou came to see Carol as a contradiction. On the one hand, she had an amiable, easy air about her—quick to laugh, always ready with an engaging, sometimes witty response. In a word, she was fun. Fun to talk to, fun to joke with, fun to be around. On the other hand, she was instinctively cautious. The obedient daughter of a preacher, she was raised to be wary of men and their intentions. Her father was fond of asking all of her suitors to come down into his basement to "see his trains." Whereupon, without turning on the lights he threatened them life and limb if they were to do anything unseemly with his daughter. As the latest in a long line, Lou received this lecture as well. He thought it might have had a strong effect on a high school–aged boy who lived in the preacher's home town. For a junior in college, however, with no attachment to her father's congregation or faith, the lecture simply raised practical roadblocks. By then, he had completely fallen for Carol Jamison. Now he knew that Mr. Jamison had to approve of Lou before Carol could fully fall for him.

He spent a lot of time with her father and his "trains."

Between dates with Carol and lectures from her dad, Lou's grade point average took a beating. But there was no turning back. He thought of Carol during class and study time anyway, so it was no good trying to rescue his grades by pulling away. Ultimately, Lou, who had been raised a nonpracticing Christian, won the trust of Carol's religiously devoted father, and he proposed. It was then that Lou learned a lesson about Carol's independence. She might have shared her father's caution, but she did not blindly act upon his approvals. When Lou first proposed, she told him she would have to think about it. He held onto the ring for five months before she finally allowed him to slip it on her finger. The moment would stay with Lou forever: "Yes, Lou, I will marry you," she suddenly told him out of the blue, as they were driving home from a church service one rainy Sunday afternoon.

"Excuse me?" Lou couldn't help from blurting.

"I'll marry you, Lou. I'll devote my life to you and to our family."

And she had.

As Lou remembered this, he knew he had not returned the single-minded devotion. Oh, his eye never wandered to other women. That was not his vice. No, his problem was not occasional lust for others, it was rather a constant lust for himself—for his own success, his own station in the world.

It had started innocuously enough with his decision to enlist in the marines and go to Vietnam. He started toying with the idea while Carol was mulling his marriage proposal. Perhaps out of fear of rejection, or maybe as a way of avoiding what ultimately would be a public embarrassment if she were to finally reject him, or still yet out of a fervent patriotism, Lou had enlisted two days before Carol surprised him with her acceptance. It would be five years before they would walk down the aisle.

That was twenty-five years ago. Their first child, Mary, was born less than a year after that, and their second, Jesse, followed two years later. Lou's first company was "born" shortly thereafter, and with it a workplace obsession that left Carol to play the part of a single parent—emotionally in any case, if not physically as well. Cory, their third child, was more than a day old before Lou made it to the hospital to see him and to see Carol. "The meetings in New York just couldn't wait," he had told her. They never could. Even though Yale Hospital in New Haven was only a ninety minute excursion from Wall Street.

Carol had been hurt by his absence, but she had by then grown used to it. Lou didn't take well to being told what to do or when to do it, so she had learned over the years not to ask much of him. The contradictory combination of her fierce devotion and steely independence is what held the family, such as it was, together. He blanched in memory of the time, ten years or so after they married, when after Carol had asked him to do something, he had asked her to come into their walk-in closet. Unsure why, she had timidly followed. Lou had then instructed her to put on a pair of his pants. She looked at him quizzically but played along. "Now Carol," he had said, "What do you notice about those pants?"

"That they're too big for me," she had said, as the waist gaped open around her.

"And never forget it!" Lou had answered emphatically, referring not to the difference in their waist sizes, but to the weight of the responsibilities Lou felt he shouldered.

He shuddered at the memory. If Carol's father had still been alive, Lou knew he would have deserved a violent meeting with his trains.

These cogitations remained with Lou the next morning as he and Carol drove in silence to Camp Moriah. As they neared the offices, he could keep his thoughts to himself no longer. "Carol, I'm so sorry," he said. "Deeply sorry."

"For what?"

"For everything." He shook his head pathetically. "For not loving you as you have deserved to be loved. For not being there for you as you have always been there for me."

Carol didn't say anything for a minute. Her eyes started to water. "You've been there, Lou," she finally said. "Sometimes you've been other places as well, that may be true. But you've always come home to me. Many women are not so fortunate.

Not many can say that they've never had to worry, but I've never had to worry about you, Lou. Whatever else you might be devoted to, I've always known that you were devoted to me too."

"But it shouldn't have been a 'me too,'" Lou said. "That isn't good enough. Then he set his jaw. "I'm going to make it up to you. I promise."

After a moment's silence, Carol said, "You're not the only one who needs to apologize."

"What do you mean?"

"You know what I mean," she said. "I've been there for you, I suppose, but my heart hasn't necessarily been there. I've been blaming silently for years."

"But you've had every right to," Lou defended her truthfully.

"Have I?" She turned to him. "The more I've become consumed with how my own needs aren't being met, the larger those needs have become, until I think I have numbed myself to the needs of others—to your needs, to Cory's."

"There you go beating yourself up again, Carol."

"No, Lou, beating myself up is what I have quietly been doing for years now. I'm not beating myself up now, I'm just finally noticing the internal fight."

"But all you've done for years is meet everyone else's needs, Carol. You've never lived for yourself at all."

Carol smiled weakly. "That's what I've been telling myself too, Lou, but it hasn't been true. I see that now." And then she added, "I've been hating you, Lou."

This rocked him.

"Hating me?" he repeated lamely.

"Blaming you, in all kinds of subtle ways." She paused. "Have I dutifully performed the household work? Yes. But that's just a behavior, don't you see? Every time I've cleaned the house, I think I've buried myself a level deeper in self-pity. And I have spent years now feeling guilty for not feeling about you the way I know I should. It's been a downward spiral."

Lou didn't know what to say. "So what are you going to do?" he finally asked.

"I don't know for sure. I hope to get more help with that today."

At that, the conversation went quiet, and Lou and Carol pondered their situations in silence. Two minutes later, they arrived at Camp Moriah.

It was time to go deeper.

16 · A Gift in Wartime

"So, how was everyone's evening?" Avi asked with a big smile once the group had seated themselves in the room.

Lou looked around at them and was surprised to discover that he felt at home in the room, as if among friends. *Yes, that is what they have become,* he thought. *Pettis, the fellow vet and clear-minded student. Elizabeth, the high-minded Brit with subtle humor and surprising self-honesty. Ria and Miguel, the oddly matched couple with an ongoing battle over the dishes. Jenny's quiet and timid parents, Carl and Teri. Even Gwyn, Lou's blustery counterpart, who had accused Lou of being racist.* Lou started chuckling at the realization that he was even glad to see Gwyn.

"Lou, what's so funny?" Avi asked.

"Oh nothing," he smiled. "It's just good to see everyone this morning, that's all."

"Even me?" Gwyn asked with a wry smile.

"*Especially* you, Gwyn," Lou laughed.

In the comfort of the moment it was easy to forget how much had changed since the morning before.

"So how do we get out of the box?" Avi asked rhetorically. "How can our hearts turn from war to peace? That is the question for today."

"Good, because I sure want the answer," Lou said.

"Actually, Lou, you have already lived the answer," Avi replied.

"No, I don't think so," Lou smirked.

"Sure you have. Just compare how you are seeing and feeling about everyone here today to how you were seeing and feeling about them yesterday morning."

It was as if someone suddenly turned on a bank of lights Lou had grown accustomed to seeing without. His thoughts and feelings about this room and the people in it had changed. He could see it. But how?

Lou verbalized his internal question: "You're right. Things seem different to me this morning. But why?" he asked. "How?"

"Do you mind if I tell you a story?" Avi asked.

"Please."

"Do you remember my stuttering and my suicide attempts?"

Lou and the rest nodded.

"I'd like to tell you what happened. To do that, I need to go back to 1973."

Avi started pacing across the front of the room. "I celebrated my fifteenth birthday on October 5, 1973," he began. "The next day was Yom Kippur, or the Day of Atonement, the holiest day on the Hebrew calendar. It's a day of prayer and fasting in Israel, a day when everyone—even Israel's defense forces—gather at home or in their synagogues in religious observance.

"Egypt and Syria launched a surprise attack that day at precisely 2:00 p.m.—Egypt from the south and Syria from the north. I'll never forget the piercing shriek of sirens that called the reservists from their worship and into uniform. My father, himself a reservist, raced from our Tel Aviv home within minutes. His unit was mobilized to the north, to fight back the Syrians along the Golan Heights.

"That was the last time I ever saw him."

Avi paused for a moment and then continued. "As a young boy raised on the David-and-Goliath-like tales of the Six Day War, I expected him home within the week. But he was killed in a mortar attack three days later—one of many casualties in a place aptly called the Valley of Tears.

"My best friend was an Israeli Arab named Hamish. His father and mine worked at the same company. We met at an event the company threw for employee families. He lived in Jaffa, not too far from my home on the south side of Tel Aviv. We got together as often as we could.

"Of all the children I associated with in my youth, Hamish was the only one who never made fun of my stutter. It wasn't just that he never made outward fun of me, it was that I knew he never thought ill of me inwardly either. After all, what were a few garbled words between friends?

"When Hamish heard about my father, he came to grieve with me. But angrily I sent him away. I'll never forget the scene: Hamish, his head bowed reverently at my door while I forced out a string of butchered obscenities and blamed him for my father's death. I blamed him, my best friend, my playmate from my youth. He killed my father—he and those who believed and looked like him. That is what I said.

"I shook in rage as he, still bowing, retreated from my doorstep, turned silently away, and then walked forlornly down the street and out of my life.

"Two of the most important people in my life were suddenly gone—one a Jew, taken out by an Arab's weapon, and another an Arab, banished by the verbal bullets of a Jew.

"There was another casualty, of course. As we've learned, such a turn from the humanity of another requires extensive justification. I began to exterminate in my mind a whole portion of the human race. Arabs were bloodsuckers, cowards, thieves, murderers—mere dogs who rightfully deserved death and were let to live only by the good graces of the Israeli people. What I didn't realize until years later is that whenever I dehumanize another, I necessarily dehumanize all that is human—including myself. What began as a hate for Arabs developed into a hate for any Jews who refused to share my hate for Arabs and nearly ended with a level of self-loathing that left me in a pool of blood on a bathroom floor in Tempe, Arizona.

"But that's how I met Yusuf.

"My mother, frightened by the depths I sank to after my father's death, had sent me to the United States in the summer of 1974, to live with her brother. It was here that I learned to hate two other groups: first, the religious Jews, represented by my observant uncle, who insisted on looking to God when it was obvious that God, if there was one, was looking the other way; and second, the affluent Americans with all their toys and commercial gadgets, who looked askance at the stuttering teenager who was forced to wear a kippah, or skullcap.

"I wrestled with my stuttering as an act of survival and self-defense and finally was able to gain a kind of conscious control over it by the time I enrolled at Arizona State University. But I was alone—cut off from the humanity that walked and talked and drove by me on every side. I was a solitary human soul.

"You might think that that would have paid off in good grades," he chuckled, breaking some of the tension of his story, "giving me plenty of time to study. But like many who are lonely, I was more preoccupied with others than were those who lived to socialize. You see, I was never really alone, even when I had physically separated myself from others, because I was thinking about my father, my people, the Arabs, and Hamish. Everyone I hated was always with me, even when I was alone. They had to be, for I had to remember what and why I hated in order to remind myself to stay away from them.

"After my second suicide attempt and a brief stay in the hospital, I was released to ponder my future. At the time it seemed bleak. I had been placed on probation after my first year at ASU, and my second-year grades were even worse. I expected to be expelled. One day in early May, I received a letter from the provost's office—my expulsion notice.

"Or so I thought. In reality, it was a final, merciful lifeline. I was being invited to enroll in a forty-day survival program being run by one of the university's faculty—an Arab by the name of Yusuf al-Falah." He extended his arm toward Yusuf, who nodded ever so slightly in response.

"Which of course meant that I wasn't going to do it," Avi continued. "I would sooner be expelled than be forced to spend forty days and nights with a hate-monger, which is what I, as a hate-monger myself, assumed he must be. And I told my mother as much, who by then had moved to the States herself.

"'You will enroll in this program, Avi,' she scolded me, 'or you will no longer be my son. And don't think I don't mean it,' she continued. 'You've twice already tried to remove yourself from my life, and something in you stole the boy I once knew some four years ago anyway. So I will make it easy on you, Avi: if you turn from this opportunity—this gift you do not deserve—because of some blind grudge you hold toward someone you have never met, then you will not be my son. You certainly would be no son of your father.'"

Avi paused in his telling to take in a deep breath. "And so I went," he said. "I went to live with my enemy."

The group waited for him to continue.

"So what happened?" Gwyn asked.

"Would you mind?" Yusuf asked permission of Avi.

"No, not at all," Avi said. "Please."

Yusuf walked to the front of the room. "To give you a feeling for what happened, perhaps it would help to tell you about something that happened here yesterday—with Carl and Teri's daughter, Jenny."

Jenny! Lou thought to himself. He couldn't believe he'd let her slip from his mind.

"Carl, Teri," Yusuf asked, "would you mind if I shared with the group how you brought Jenny here?"

Carl fidgeted beneath the attention that suddenly came his way but said, "That would be fine."

"You're sure about that?"

"Yes, go ahead."

"Teri?"

"Sure, it's fine."

"Okay then," Yusuf began, turning to the rest of the group. "When Jenny climbed in her parents' car yesterday morning, she didn't know she was being transported to a treatment program. Now you know we don't recommend that, but it happens. Jenny's brother was in the car as well. He held Jenny so she wouldn't bolt from the moving vehicle when her parents broke the news. You of course saw the state Jenny was in after she got out of her brother's clutches and bolted across the street. You may not have noticed that she was without shoes. That may not seem vital at 9:00 a.m. But it's a different story when the Arizona sun begins to heat the city pavement, I can assure you. Even in April.

"As I mentioned yesterday afternoon, Jenny ran shortly after we began our session, and two of our young people set off after her. What I'd like to tell you about is what happened over the next few hours as they followed her."

"Few hours?" Lou asked.

"Yes. The young people who followed her are named Mei Li and Mike. They were each once students in our program but now work with us. Mei Li is twenty, and Mike, twenty-two.

"In fact, they are with us this morning," he said, extending his hand toward the back of the room.

The group whirled their heads around.

Mei Li and Mike, each of them comfortable in worn khakis and T-shirts, smiled back at them. Mike slipped the bandana from his head and tipped it, like ball players tip their caps. Mei Li waved sheepishly.

"Would you mind coming up and sharing what happened yesterday?" Yusuf asked.

They smiled and nodded and walked to the front.

"Well," Mike began, "Jenny took off running about fifteen minutes after you came into the building. She had a few blocks head start when Mei Li and I took off after her. We called to Jenny as we caught up, but she yelled at us, and started screaming about how her parents had betrayed her.

"Sorry," he said to Carl and Teri, when he realized what he had said. He winced slightly and ducked his head in apology.

Carl shook his head and waved the concern away with a perfunctory flick of his wrist. "Don't worry about it," he said.

"Jenny was crying," Mei Li chimed in. "Nothing we said helped; maybe made it worse even. She began running faster and jumping walls trying to ditch us."

"She runs steeplechase," her mother offered, almost in apology.

"Figures," Mei Li laughed. "We did our best to keep up though."

"And to keep up a conversation," Mike added. "We continued that way—jogging after her and trying to talk—for quite a while. But then Mei Li noticed something."

"What?" Teri asked.

"That Jenny's feet were bleeding. So we asked her if it would be okay if we called someone to bring some shoes."

"And?" Teri asked.

Mike shook his head. "She wouldn't have any of it."

Teri sighed.

"But then Mei Li sat down," Mike continued, "and began removing her own shoes. 'Take mine then, Jenny,' she said. 'Your feet are beat up; mine are fine. Please.' But Jenny called her something I'd rather not repeat and kept running."

Jenny's father, Carl, shook his head in resignation.

"Didn't matter though," Mike continued. "Mei Li took off her shoes anyway."

Teri and Carl looked at them inquiringly.

"Mike did the same," Mei Li added. "Dropped down on the spot and took his shoes off too. Then we tried to catch up to her."

"Barefoot?" Lou asked.

"Yes," Mei Li answered.

"For how long?"

"Oh," she said, "another three hours or so."

"*Three hours!* Barefoot on the pavement? In Phoenix?"

"Yes."

"But *why?*"

"That is the question," Yusuf jumped in. "And I bet at the time Mei Li and Mike couldn't have even articulated the reason. They just knew it was the thing to do."

"But it doesn't make any sense," Lou retorted. "She didn't want their shoes. All they did was beat themselves up."

"Actually, Lou," Yusuf responded, "it makes the deepest sense in the world. And while they certainly inconvenienced themselves, their act accomplished something of great importance."

"Then what? What did it accomplish?"

"What indeed."

17 · *Marching Bootless*

"No, seriously, what did it accomplish?" Lou persisted. "What good did this do—taking off their shoes?"

"It isn't so much what good it did," Yusuf responded, "as what good it invited."

"Okay, then, what good did it invite?"

Yusuf looked at Mei Li and Mike. "Do you want to speak to that?"

"Sure," Mei Li said. She looked at Lou. "I'm not sure what good it invited, Mr. Herbert," she began.

How does she know who I am? Lou wondered.

"But I know what happened—to Jenny," she continued. "She decided on her own to enroll in the program. And I bet you wouldn't have predicted that."

"No," Lou agreed, his eyebrows rising in surprise, "I can't say that I would have." Then he added, "How did that happen?"

"Well, after a few hours, we finally ended up at a mall. And Jenny ran into one of her friends. She started telling her what her parents had done to her and about this program they had tried to take her to. She mentioned that we worked for that program as well and that we had been following her for most of the day.

"The friend then looked down at our feet, which were all bloody, and asked the question you just asked, Mr. Herbert. She said: 'Barefoot? You've been running around the city barefoot?'

"'Yeah,' Jenny chuckled back at her.

"The friend then looked at us and back at Jenny and then said, 'I don't know, Jenny, this program sounds like it might be okay. Maybe you should give it a try.'

"We talked for a while together after that, until her friend had to go. After she left, Jenny turned to us and said, 'Okay then, tell me more about this Camp Moriah.'

"We answered everything she wanted to know. We told her about Yusi and Avi, about the wilderness we go to, and how we live off the land and how fun and interesting it is—how liberating, really. She didn't believe us about the liberating part," Mei Li laughed. "But she kept listening. And after a while of talking about it, you know what she said?"

The group hung on the answer.

"She said, 'Okay. I'll go.' Just that. She wasn't thrilled, certainly. More resigned than anything, I think. But she was willing. And then during our ride back here together, just before we pulled into the parking lot, she said, 'I'm sorry for all the things I said to you today. And for your feet.' She was genuinely sorry. I know, because I could see the water in her eyes.

"So, Mr. Herbert, did taking our shoes off have anything to do with Jenny now being safely and willingly out on the trail? I don't know for sure. You'd have to ask Jenny. But I do know one thing for certain: I know what taking my shoes off meant for me. It was a way of joining Jenny in her world, which is something we always try to do here. It's a way we create space for helping people to get out of the box. So, for example, when we go out on the trail and the youth have nothing but a food pack and a poncho, we too have nothing more than the same food pack and poncho."

"Unless," Mike jumped in, "for safety reasons we have to have something else—a radio, for example, or a first-aid kit."

"Right," Mei Li agreed. "There are those differences. But we keep them to a minimum. Because if the kids had nothing but cornmeal to eat, for example, but I pulled out a candy bar for myself, how would that be treating them? Or if they had to sleep on the hard ground while I had an inflatable mattress, how would *that* be treating them?"

"As objects," came Miguel's gravelly voice, surprising almost everyone in the room.

"Right," Mei Li agreed. "I would be seeing myself as better than and more deserving than them. So how do you think that would invite them to see and treat me?"

"Same way," Miguel answered again.

"Exactly," Mei Li answered. "Joining the youth in their hardships helps them because it helps us not to invite their hearts to go to war.

"So, Mr. Herbert," Mei Li continued, looking at Lou once more, "did it make a difference to Jenny? I don't know. But it made a difference to me. It helped me keep a heart at peace. And I think that might have made a difference to her. Like Yusuf and Avi always tell us, we can't be agents of peace until our own hearts are at peace."

Lou sat stunned. Here was a twenty-year-old girl, probably less than two years removed from high school, and herself a delinquent in years past, who seemed to have a command of life that Lou himself knew he had not yet approached.

"Thank you, Mei Li and Mike," Yusuf said.

Turning back to the group, he added, "Do you think your children are in good hands now?"

"I'll say," Gwyn answered, with others adding similar sentiments.

"Thanks," Lou nodded at Mei Li and then at Mike.

"Sure."

"Well, then," Yusuf continued, after the two of them had left. "You've now met our secret weapon—the young people here at Camp Moriah who work the miracles in your children's lives. I'd like to discuss something that follows from what they just taught us.

"Most wars between individuals are of the 'cold' rather than the 'hot' variety—lingering resentment, for example, grudges long held, resources clutched to rather than shared, help not offered. These are the acts of war that most threaten our homes and workplaces. And the principles Mei Li shared with us apply no less in those environments than they do here on the trail with your youth. Think about our workplaces, for example. Think of the privileges we may retain for ourselves while we apply other standards to those who work for us—privileges regarding vacation time, for example, the choice parking spot, the special perks, the public spotlight, the differences between what we have to do to get something to happen and what everyone else in our organization has to do. Which of these are necessary or unavoidable, and which of them do we retain because we think we are better than others, more vital, and deserve special treatment?"

"But what if you are?" Lou challenged, although good-naturedly.

"More vital, you mean?"

"Yes."

"Then I would start wondering what special accommodations are vital in order for me to perform my vital function, and what perks are simply personal indulgences. In other words, which of them are the candy bars and inflatable mattresses, and which of them are the radios and first-aid kits?"

"But why should that be the question?" Lou countered. "If I've worked all my life to get to where I am, shouldn't I be able to enjoy it?"

Yusuf smiled, clearly enjoying the exchange. "Yes, Lou. Absolutely. And that's just the point, isn't it, because everyone else wants to enjoy the fruits of their labors as well. The question for you as the leader is whether you are going to create an environment that is as enjoyable for your people as it is for you—a place that they are as excited about and devoted to as you are. The best leaders are those whom people want to follow. We have a different word for people whom others follow only because of force or need. We call them tyrants."

Tyrants. The word echoed uncomfortably in Lou's ear, for it was what one of Lou's fired executives, Jack Taylor, had called him. *No doubt what Cory would say as well,* he reflected.

What Lou didn't say was that no one who pulled up at Zagrum Company would have the least question which car was Lou's, which office was Lou's, which desk was Lou's, which furnishings were Lou's. And Lou certainly played by a different set of rules than the rest. Others had to get his approval for any expenditure over $2,000, for example. He, on the other hand, could spend whatever he wanted whenever he wanted. *But I'm the boss!* he defended himself.

"So what are you saying, Yusuf?" he challenged. "That I don't deserve anything extra for all that I've done? I've built the company, for heaven's sake."

"Alone?"

"Excuse me?"

"You've built the company alone?"

"No, that's not what I meant."

"No? It's what you said."

"Well it's not what I meant." Lou struggled to find the right words. "I mean that I led the building. It wouldn't have happened but for me."

"You're no doubt right, Lou. No doubt at all. So here's the question: What's more important to you now—flaunting your well-earned important status or building a team and organization that will outlive you, surpass you, grow beyond you, and ultimately thank and revere you? What do you want, Lou?"

This question brought Lou squarely back to the mutiny in the boardroom. Kate Stenarude, Jack Taylor, Nelson Mumford, Kirk Weir, Don Shilling—Lou wrote their obituaries that morning, and with them, perhaps, the obituary of his "baby," Zagrum. *Who am I kidding?* he taunted himself. *We're on the way down. No one's going to thank me, much less revere me. That devotion was reserved for Kate.*

Kate. All of a sudden her name took on new meaning. *She was one of the people,* Lou thought to himself. *That's why everyone loved her. And followed her. She didn't think she was any better—more fortunate maybe, but no better.*

"I'll be damned!" Lou blurted aloud, shaking his head. "I'll be damned."

"Excuse me?" Yusuf said.

"I just fired the one person in my company," Lou began, his eyes glassy as he spoke, "who refused to play by a different set of rules from everyone else. She treated everyone the same. Drove me crazy sometimes, the attention she would give to some of the staff—even the temps." Lou paused. "I even caught her helping the janitorial staff clean the cafeteria one day when they were shorthanded. I couldn't believe it. Thought she was wasting her time and my money. But they loved her for it," he said, shaking his head in realization. "Always made a point of parking at the far end of the lot too. Claimed she needed the exercise." It suddenly struck him that it wasn't just about the exercise.

"And I'm left with a lot of people like me," he continued, "who think they deserve the best." He shook his head in disgust. "I've had the choice parking spot for years, and the choice everything else for that matter, and look what it's gotten me. Since I fired Kate and the others, we've been in crisis. Labor has me over a barrel, everyone's worried, our production is down, our customers are wondering what's going on. And here I sit in Arizona—partly because I need to be here, and partly because I don't have a clue what to do about the mess back home. And now it comes to me: I'm the mess. That's what you're saying here—that *I'm* the mess."

"Well actually, you're the one saying that," Yusuf said sheepishly. "I didn't say that."

"That's okay, I'll say it," Elizabeth chided.

Lou was lost in his thoughts. "No wonder everyone loved and followed Kate," he continued mostly to himself. "Damn, have I ever made a mistake."

"So what are you going to do about it?"

"I don't know," he said honestly.

"Perhaps Kate can give you a suggestion," Yusuf answered.

"But I fired her. She's no longer with me."

"On the contrary, Lou, she's never been bigger in your mind than she is now. You might have let her go from your company, but you haven't been able to let her go from your mind. Am I wrong?"

"No, you're right," he said slumping in his chair.

"There is a reason Kate was beloved," Yusuf continued, "a reason people followed her and worked for her. And from what I've heard about Kate, I have a suspicion I know what it was."

"What?"

"Something that one of our Kates—Mei Li—just taught us. Kate created a space for people at Zagrum that was akin to the space Mei Li helped to create for Jenny. Like Mei Li, I'm betting that when Kate showed up for work each morning, she took off her shoes, or whatever the equivalent of that is in your company. In an environment that is often fearful and ego-driven, she created a space where people could give up their worries and thrive."

Yusuf waited as Lou pondered this.

"Am I right?" he finally asked.

"Yes," Lou said, his mind now far away in a building in Connecticut. "You are."

18 · *Surrender*

Yusuf tilted his head down to intercept Lou's faraway gaze. "I know that look," he said. "It's how I look when I possess no real conviction that things can ever get better. It is the look of despair and surrender."

Lou took that in and considered it. "Yeah, I suppose that is how I'm feeling," he conceded.

"It's a seductively powerful feeling," Yusuf continued, "this feeling of despairing surrender. But it's a lie."

Lou suddenly perked up. "How so?"

"Because it's assuming something that isn't true."

"What?"

"It's assuming that you're stuck—that you're doomed to continue suffering as you have been."

This was, in fact, what Lou was feeling. He slumped again in his chair.

"Just a moment ago, Lou," Yusuf began, "you said that you were the mess. Not others, but you."

"And that's supposed to make me feel better?" Lou asked forlornly.

"No," Yusuf responded, "but it should give you hope."

"How so?"

"Because if you are the mess, you can clean it. Improvement doesn't depend on others."

"But what if the mess isn't purely mine?" Lou responded sullenly. "What if the people around me are just as messed up as I am?"

Yusuf couldn't help himself: "Then you have a huge problem," he laughed out loud.

"Tell me about it." Lou shook his head pathetically.

"Actually, I'm mostly joking, Lou," Yusuf continued.

"Mostly," Elizabeth noted with a smile.

"Yes," Yusuf agreed, "mostly. Because even if it's the case that everyone at Zagrum is deeply messed up, it's still a hopeful situation."

"How do you figure?"

"Because your despair is being invited by another lie. You're assuming that nothing you can do will change them."

"But that's true," Lou countered. "I can't change them."

"Quite right."

"Then I don't understand your point."

"That's because you surrendered too early," Yusuf smiled. "While it's true we can't *make* others change, we can invite them to change. After all, didn't Mei Li help to change Jenny?"

Lou thought about Mei Li's story. "Yes, I suppose she did."

Yusuf paused briefly. "Because we are each responsible for our blaming, self-justifying boxes," he continued, "we can each be rid of them. There are no victims so far as the box is concerned, only self-made ones. And since by getting out of the box we invite the same in others, we are not even victims with respect to others the way we believe we are when we're in the box. We can begin inviting others to make the changes they need to make. In fact, that is what the best leaders and parents do. So if you surrender, Lou, you surrender to a lie. Your box will win."

"Then how?" Lou asked. "How can I fight this box I'm in?"

"The same way Avi fought his and I'm fighting mine."

"How?" Lou repeated.

"I think it might help to hear more of Avi's story," Yusuf said.

At that, Avi stood back up. "So," he began again, "the Arizona outback in the summer of '78."

Lou listened as Avi recounted his initial meeting with Yusuf, their early battles, Avi's anger at everything around him—the hills, the streams, the trees, the earth.

"But everything began to change for me," Avi continued, "during a late-night conversation with Yusuf under a clear, star-laden sky. We were about two weeks into the program at the time, and I'd barely said a word to anyone. 'You know,' Yusuf said to me, as I was lying on my back looking at the stars, 'it's the same night sky we see from Jerusalem.'

"I hesitated. But then I said, 'Yeah—the Big Dipper, the Polar Star. I remember my dad teaching me all about them.'

"At that, I recall Yusuf sitting down next to me. It might have been the first time I didn't pull away from him.

"He said, 'Tell me about your father, Avi.' And I remember launching into a flood of memories from my childhood: how my father took me on walks every day from as early as I can remember, how he taught me the history of our people, how he played soccer with me at the park, how he always cooked Saturday breakfast, how I loved to travel with him on his surveying jobs, how he always read to me before I went to bed. It was like a dam broke within me and my memories burst free. All my love for my father, the pain of his loss, and the sadness for no longer having him in my life burst through the box that had been confining my heart. My chest heaved at the loss I had suffered and at what I was then suddenly recovering: a longing to be with my father.

"Yusuf just sat there with me and listened. Although he couldn't have known it, he was something of a surrogate for my father that night. If I couldn't be with my father, it was at least helpful to be with *someone* after nearly five years of barricading myself from the world. That night was the beginning of my healing. And I will forever be grateful that it happened at the invitation of an Arab. For the blame I had heaped upon the Arab people for my father's death somehow became more difficult to maintain when it was an Arab who helped reintroduce me to my father.

"When I awoke the next morning, I willingly joined in with the others and helped with breakfast. This was a first for me. We then broke camp and began our day's journey through the bush. I remember the morning's hike well because it was the first day on the trail that I allowed myself to enjoy.

"Over the days that followed, the memories of another flooded my mind: Hamish. What a friend he had been! How gracious, pure, and good he had been to me. And I, so wicked! He had come to me in my moment of great loss, knowing how deeply I must be hurting, and wanting in some small way to help me bear my pain. He had come as an angel of comfort and goodwill, and I cast him out."

Avi reached up and wiped at his cheek.

"And as if that wasn't enough, I vilified him—with every vile word I knew. I blamed him for my father's death. Him! The bearer of mercy and love. The young boy stuck between two nations—Arab by birth and Israeli by citizenship. The boy who in the days his blood family was attacking his country, when perhaps he needed comfort most of all, came to offer his comfort to me and received pain in return for his merciful gift—mean, loathsome pain.

"*Oh Hamish!* I cried within as I walked. *What can I ever do to repay you—to belatedly return your gift in kind, to help to bear the pain I have heaped upon you, and to erase the bitterness I have inevitably invited within?*"

Avi wiped once more at his cheek.

"This question settled upon me as I trekked over the coming days. On another clear evening some ten days or so after the first, I again sat with Yusuf. This time I told him about my friend Hamish, and my violent turning away. The telling was cathartic, as I had never uttered a word of it to anyone until that moment. I had of course spent the recent days replaying the events in my mind, but until I was willing to allow another to see my transgression, I was still holding on to and hiding it. My telling turned out to be part of the healing.

"Part, but not all. For the telling nourished within me the seed that had been looking to take hold and grow: I knew in the telling that it wasn't enough in this case merely to feel sorry. Seeing Hamish as I once again did, I felt the desire and need to reach out to him.

"'What can I do for him?' I asked Yusuf.

"'Do you feel the need to do something for him?' he asked.

"'It is what my heart is telling me, yes,' I answered.

"'Then what do you feel you should do?'

"'That's what I am asking *you*,' I responded.

"'Ah,' he said, 'but it is your life and your friend and your heart, is it not? I cannot tell you what you need to do. Only you would know that.'

"*Then what?* I wondered to myself.

"'Maybe you should ponder the question as you walk over the coming days,' Yusuf said, as if reading my thoughts.

"And I did. On the third morning, we came upon a spectacular plant called a century plant. Its stalk was probably thirty feet tall. The century plant lives fifteen to twenty-five years. However, it shoots up a stalk and flowers only in the last year of its life. The energy it takes to grow the stalk ends up killing the plant. When the stalk falls over, it showers seeds on the ground, giving life to a new generation. The low-lying base of the plant is commonly seen in the deserts of Arizona and elsewhere. But the once-in-a-lifetime nature of the stalk, and its determination to grow skyward from rocky, dry soil, lends it an air of authority and hope. Because of the seeds it cradles, every stalk that rises offers the desert the promise of future life.

"I had learned about the plant since joining the survival course and had seen various specimens over the first few weeks. This time, however, when I happened upon one in full flower, something hit me: I had received the gift of a once-in-a-lifetime friend; a friend and friendship that had flourished despite the difficulty of the environment in which we lived. It was of course a friendship that lived close to the ground—like the base of the century plant, mostly unnoticed. Yet before it could come of age and shoot its flower skyward as a beacon of hope to the desert, I had hacked at its roots and condemned it to death. Towering before me was a surrogate: this plant was now rising as Hamish and I could have risen had I not deserted him.

"I reached up to the lowest of its branches and snapped off a seed. I wrapped up the seed, symbolic both of what I had killed and what I hoped yet could rise to life, and placed it in my pocket. That evening, I laid my soul bare in a letter to Hamish, apologizing for my inhumanity toward him and for the pain I had inevitably caused. I offered the seed as a symbol both of what we once had and of what I hoped we could yet recover.

"I didn't know whether Hamish or his family still lived in the same little home, but his house number was my only connection to the life I had once known with him. The weekly mail run arrived in our camp two days later. My letter and the century plant's seed started their journey from the desert soils of Arizona to the deserts of the Middle East, hopefully to find a young Palestinian Arab still in good health and retaining a spirit that had not been irretrievably damaged by the violence of some years before."

At that, Avi stopped.

"So what happened?" Gwyn asked. "Did you hear from Hamish?"

"No," he said. "I never heard from him."

There was the hint of a gasp in the room, as this revelation was neither what they had expected nor hoped.

"That's sad," Gwyn said. "Do you know what happened to him?"

"Yes. I have learned since that his family moved about two years after I came to the States. They moved to the north of Israel to a town called Maalot-Tarshiha. But he was killed about five years later. He was among the civilians killed by rocket attacks from Lebanon prior to the Lebanon War of 1982."

"Oh how sad," Gwyn whispered.

"Yes," Avi nodded as he looked down at the ground.

"Did he ever receive your letter?" Elizabeth asked.

Avi shook his head. "I don't know. There's no way to know." He looked back up at the group. "I didn't learn of his whereabouts until after his death."

"What a pity if he never received it," Carol said.

"Yes," Avi agreed, his face slack with sorrow. "I wonder about it all the time—about the pain I caused him and about whether my letter helped to relieve it in any way."

"But writing the letter helped *you*," Pettis offered.

"By helping to heal my own heart, you mean?" Avi asked. "Yes."

"You're right," he agreed. "Even if the letter didn't reach Hamish, it reached me. That's true. It was for me an outward expression of an inward recovery of friendship. Hamish may not have received it, but in writing it I finally received him and began to receive others like him."

"Like Arabs, you mean?" Gwyn asked. "Like Yusuf and others?"

"Yes. And Americans and Jews and my family and myself—everyone I had gone to war against. For you see, every human face includes all others. This means that I spite my own face with every nose I desire to cut off. We separate from each other at our own peril."

19 • *Locating the Peace Within*

"Lou," Avi said, "a few minutes ago you asked how you can get out of the boxes you find yourself in—out of the blame, the self-justification, the internal warring, the apparent stuckness."

"Yes," Lou said.

"From this story I've just shared, I'd like to highlight for you what I believe were the keys to my being released from the captivity of my own boxes—the getting-out-of-the-box process, as it were."

Lou nodded in both assent and anticipation.

"First of all," Avi began, "you need to realize something about the box. Since the box is just a metaphor for how I am in relationship with another person, I can be both in and out of the box at the same time, just in different directions. That is, I can be blaming and justifying toward my wife, for example, and yet be living straightforwardly toward Yusuf, or vice versa. Given the hundreds of relationships I have at any given time, even if I am deeply in a box toward one person, I am nearly always out of the box toward someone else."

"Okay," Lou said pensively, wondering why this might be significant.

"Which is why," Avi continued, "we can recognize we are in the box to begin with. When we are noticing we are in the box, it is because we are noticing that we aren't feeling and seeing in one direction like we are in another. We are able to recognize the difference because the difference is within us. Which is to say that we have out-of-the-box places within us—relationships and memories that are not twisted and distorted by blame and self-justification."

"Okay," Lou said, "but what does that have to do with getting out of the box when we're feeling stuck?"

"It has to do with it because it means we are not stuck."

"Huh?"

"Think of that night with Yusuf under the stars," Avi continued. "It turns out that I had a wealth of out-of-the-box memories regarding my father. Once I allowed myself to find my way to those memories, a lot of things started to look and feel different."

"But you could have made your way to those memories any time in the prior five years but evidently didn't," Lou said. "What made you do it *that* night?"

"Good question," Avi responded. "I've asked myself the same thing many times."

"And?"

"And I think the answer lies in the ideas Mei Li and Mike shared with us—ideas that were embedded in the efforts Yusuf made with me and the others who were on the survival course. Remember how Mei Li talked about the importance of doing everything in her power to make the environment invitational toward peace? That is one of our precepts here. The biggest help in finding my way forward and out of the box was finding an out-of-the-box place, or vantage point, within me. In order to give me the best chance at finding such a vantage point within me, Yusuf helped to create an out-of-the-box place around me."

"And how did he do that?"

"By first being out of the box toward me himself. For you see, when he approached me that night under the stars, the conversation never would have gone as it did had I felt the blame of his box over the preceding days. I was like Jenny, and Yusuf was like

Mike and Mei Li. I was looking to take offense at slights real and imagined. When real offenses wane, however, it gets increasingly harder to keep manufacturing them in one's mind. Despite my early resistance toward Yusuf, he didn't resist me back. He helped to create for me, as it were, an out-of-the-box place—a vantage point from where I could ponder my life in a new way free from the blame and self-justification of the box. When I remembered in that way, I was free to remember a past that my blaming self-justification had kept me from remembering. I was free to see a different past along with a different present and future. I was freed from the limitations and distortions of the box."

"So what is the getting-out-of-the-box process you alluded to earlier?" Lou asked.

"I've already given you the first two parts," Avi answered. At that, Avi turned to the board and wrote the following:

RECOVERING INNER CLARITY AND PEACE
(FOUR PARTS)
Getting out of the box

1. Look for the signs of the box (blame, justification, horribilization, common box styles, etc.).
2. Find an out-of-the-box place (out-of-the-box relationships, memories, activities, places, etc.).

"First," Avi said, as he turned from the board, "I should be on the lookout for blame and justification—for the signs that I might be in a box. I can be on the lookout for signs of the various common boxes, for example—ways I'm feeling better-than, or entitled, or worse-than, or anxious to be seen-as.

"Then when I feel stuck in the box and desire to get out, I can find an out-of-the-box place—some place within me that is unencumbered by these boxes."

"And that's what you found that night with Yusuf?" Lou asked.

"Yes, and in the memories that then came of my father."

"But what about when I'm not on the trail with Yusuf?" Lou asked earnestly. "How can I find an out-of-the-box place when all hell is breaking loose around me?"

Lou wasn't trying to trip Avi up at this point. He simply knew from past experience that whatever he was learning from this likely would be swept away and forgotten at the first sign of difficulty. His lunchtime conversation with John Rencher the day before was exhibit number one of this. He wanted to find some toeholds for himself—things he could remember and latch onto when he felt the walls of the box erecting themselves around him.

"Actually," Avi answered, "since we all have out-of-the-box places within us, finding one is not difficult so long as we remember to do it. For example, you might try to identify the people toward whom you are generally and currently out of the box. Names will come to mind, and simply thinking about your experiences with those people can take you to a vantage point from where the world seems different than it did the moment before."

Lou nodded to himself. His oldest child, Mary, had just this kind of impact on Lou. She seemed to calm him simply by her presence. It had been that way between them almost since the day she was born. He used to take her on walks to clear his mind after a hard day, and they formed a bond. He read to her every night when she was young, and the soothing relationship they formed had lingered into the present. His next child, Jesse, didn't have quite the same calming influence. Lou had always driven him hard, whether in schoolwork or sports, and their relationship had a kind of striving intensity about it as a result. But Lou was fiercely proud of Jesse. Was this too an out-of-the-box place? He wasn't sure. "If you needed to," Avi added, "you might call or go to one of these people merely to have a conversation or perhaps to ask for help with the struggle you are having.

"Or you might try thinking about the people who have had the greatest influence for good in your life and why," he continued.

Lou suddenly found himself thinking about Carol and about her steady, devoted influence. "Very often," Avi's voice continued, "simply the memory of those people can take you to a different vantage point.

"Or maybe there was a time," he continued, "when someone treated you kindly—especially when you didn't deserve it."

Lou remembered his father's response when he had dumped their new car into the Hudson. "Such memories can be helpful to me when I find that I am in the box railing against someone I don't think deserves to be treated kindly," Avi said.

"Or maybe there is a particular book or book passage that has a powerful effect on you," he continued, "a writing that invites you out of the box." Lou thought of *The Hiding Place* and Jacques Lusseyran's autobiography, *And There Was Light*. These were each accounts of people who despite terrible hardships found ways not to be bitter.

"Or maybe an activity or place that does the same," Avi continued. "Maybe some location that brings back memories of when all was right, for example. For me, I have discovered that Frank Sinatra music, of all things, invites me to an out-of-the-box place! It has this effect on me, I believe, because I began listening to Sinatra when I used to rock our youngest child,

Lydia, to sleep. So for me, Sinatra invites me back to the memories of those times—unencumbered memories that give me the chance to think and feel more clearly in the present.

"This all sounds fairly basic, but most people who are trying to find their way out of conflict and bitterness never think to do it. Finding themselves stuck in bitterness, it never occurs to them that they have access to unbitter places in every moment.

"Once we find our way to such a place, we are ready for the next step in the getting-out-of-the-box process. We can now, by virtue of the out-of-the-box space we have found, ponder our difficult situations anew, from a perspective of peace and clarity." At that, Avi added a third item to the process he was outlining on the board.

RECOVERING INNER CLARITY AND PEACE
(FOUR PARTS)
Getting out of the box

1. Look for the signs of the box (blame, justification, horribilization, common box styles, etc.).
2. Find an out-of-the-box place (out-of-the-box relationships, memories, activities, places, etc.).
3. Ponder the situation anew (i.e., from this out-of-the-box perspective).

"What does pondering the situation anew mean?" Pettis asked. "And how do you do it, exactly?"

"Could I speak to that, Avi?" Yusuf said.

"Of course. Go ahead."

Yusuf came up to the front. "What does it mean, you ask? It means that once you find an out-of-the-box vantage point, you are now in a position to think new thoughts about situations that have troubled you. Because you will be thinking about them from a new perspective, you will be able to access thoughts and ideas that may have eluded you while you were trying to think about the situation from within the box.

"Avi found that kind of perspective," he continued, "under a star-filled sky. This may not be an out-of-the-box place for you, but Avi's point is that something will be. You need only to identify the relationships, places, memories, activities, book passages, and so on, that have that kind of power for you, and then remember to search them out when you feel war rising within you. When you've accessed such a place—an internal vantage point where peace remains—you can begin to ponder your challenges anew."

"But how?" Pettis asked.

"By learning to ask some questions."

"What questions?"

"Queries I began learning in a grassy Connecticut park," Yusuf answered. "When canisters of tear gas were exploding around me."

20 · Finding Outward Peace

"Connecticut?" Lou asked in interest, as it was his home. "And tear gas?"

"Yes," Yusuf answered. He looked contemplatively at the group for a moment. "Avi shared his story of coming to the States. Perhaps it is time I shared mine as well.

"As you'll recall from yesterday, I ended up in Bethlehem when Jordan annexed the West Bank. I began my hustling of Westerners and, as it turns out, my lessons in English when I was about eight. That would have been around 1951. Unlike Avi, I didn't have any friends from across the ethnic divide, which probably wouldn't surprise you given my antipathy toward Mordechai Lavon. In fact, I spent most of my teenage years dreaming of revenge for the murder of my father. This desire had fertile ground in which to grow, as a kind of nationalistic fever started to burn among the Palestinian people beginning in the fifties and continuing into the sixties.

"In 1957, at the age of fourteen, I joined a youth movement known as the Young Lions for Freedom. This group was an informal offshoot of student unions of Palestinians that began emerging in the region's universities in the 1950s. The younger brothers of these students, longing to attach themselves to the causes of their elders, hatched mirror organizations among their neighborhood clans. Ours was such an organization, patterned after the foremost of the student unions, which was located at Cairo University and headed by an engineering student named Yasir Arafat."

Eyebrows raised at the name.

"Yes, one and the same," Yusuf said.

"I quickly distinguished myself as a leader in the organization," he continued. "When I was just sixteen, I was invited to Kuwait to meet with the newly established leaders—Arafat one of the chief among them—of a movement that called itself Harakat At-Tahiri Al-Filistimiya, or the Palestinian National Liberation Movement. Known more popularly as Fatah, the reverse acronym of its formal name, the organization's goal, stated clearly in its founding documents, was to replace the State of Israel in its entirety with a Palestinian State through means of armed revolution. It was an intoxicating vision for a young man bent on revenge.

"I returned from Kuwait looking forward to the annihilation of Israel. It was only a matter of time; I was going to get my revenge against an entire people. I was giddy with anticipation and happiness.

"My mother, however, did not share my joy. She distrusted the messengers that would drop notes by my house at all hours of the night and began first to intercept and then to destroy the communications. 'I will not lose first my husband and then my only son too!' she yelled at me. 'The answer to the tragedy of Deir Yassin is not simply to swap the identity of the parties. You will not take up arms against the Israelis unless they first take up arms against you!'

"'But they have, Mother,' I pointed out, 'they have taken up arms; they have joined league with the West and are assembling the most powerful arsenal in the region.'

"'What do you know of arms and politics!' she snapped back at me. 'You are only a child with his head either in the clouds or buried in the sand. And as my child, you will not enter into league with these bandits of the night,' which is what she called the movement's messengers.

"'Then as my father's child, I *will*,' I shot back, knowing there would be no retribution for my impudence. 'I must.'

"And so I did. I began to act as the cell leader for Fatah in the greater Jerusalem area. This was heady stuff for a young man. As it turns out, too heady. In 1962, after I had built a grassroots network of some five thousand committed and loyal fedayeen, a nephew of Arafat moved in and took over the region. I was officially placed as second in command. Everyone in the organization knew the truth, however: I had been stripped of my power.

"This was humiliating to me, but my hatred for the Zionist Jews outstripped the humiliation, and I stayed on as a loyal foot soldier. I looked forward to our victory even in my diminished role.

"The apparent final push to victory began in the spring of 1967. In mid-May, Egypt mobilized one hundred thousand soldiers along Israel's southwestern border and declared that the Straits of Tiran would be closed to ships bound to and from Israel. President Nasser of Egypt then announced his intention to destroy Israel.

"In response, the Arab world became gripped with a kind of anticipatory hysteria. Arab forces from around the region were mobilized on all sides so that by the end of May, Israel was surrounded by an Arab legion force of some 250,000 troops, 2,000 tanks, and 700 military aircraft. I joined a battalion that had taken up a strategic position at Latrun, one of the westernmost locations in the Jordanian-occupied West Bank.

"Latrun was located on the highway between Tel Aviv and Jerusalem, the main artery in Israel. It overlooked the Jerusalem corridor, a stretch of Israeli-controlled land that fingered its way to the western parts of Jerusalem but was surrounded by Jordanian forces on the ridges to the north and the south. Latrun would be a key position from which the corridor would be first cut off from the rest of Israel and then captured. It would also be the focal point of the Arab legion's move down the foothills and across the coastal plains to Tel Aviv. I wanted to be part of the eradication of Israel's heart—both Israeli-controlled Western Jerusalem and Tel Aviv. There was no better place than Latrun.

"But you perhaps know what happened. Avi alluded to it earlier. On the morning of June 5, 1967, Israel launched a surprise preemptive strike against Egypt's planes and airfields, decimating them in a rout. They soon took out Jordanian and Syrian air power as well, leaving us without protection from the air. We received the command to break into Israeli territory shortly thereafter. But our supply routes were quickly cut off, and the mountains that had been our protection to the east now made our escape impossible. Before night fell, we knew we had been beaten. Jordan agreed to a cease-fire two days later, and the war ended in Israel's total victory just six days after it had begun. When I returned home to Bethlehem, Jordan had been pushed back to the east of the River Jordan; Israel had captured the entire West Bank!

"What followed was a crisis of confidence in the Arab world. A bitter despair swept through the Palestinian people as the Jordanians pulled back within their borders. We were left behind with those we viewed as our captors. We had been abandoned and imprisoned yet again.

"The Fatah network scrambled to regain its footing under the new reality, but we had lost our confidence and along with it much of our hope. Whatever battles lay ahead, I knew they would be much longer than I had hoped. I was not to have a leading role in them in any case. So I started looking for other battles. Battles that could give me release from the daily reminder of our failure as a people and from the gnawing hate I was beginning to carry toward my own—who had, after all, removed me from power and squandered our great opportunity."

Yusuf paused.

"So where did you look?" Pettis asked. "To what other battles?"

"At first I began to look to other Arab nations—to Egypt, for example, to Syria, to Iraq. I looked for some pro-Arab cause that I could attach myself to. Something with promise. Something to give me some kind of hope against Israel."

"So your heart was at war," Lou said slyly. "You were in the box."

Yusuf looked at him, and smiled. "Yes, Lou, I certainly was. In a box likely larger and darker than any you have ever been tempted to enter."

"Careful now," Lou warned. "I have a better-than box. Don't go trying to make your box bigger than mine."

Everyone in the room burst out laughing.

After the laughter subsided, Elizabeth asked, "So did you find what you were looking for? Did you find a battle to take up elsewhere in the Arab world?"

"I found battles everywhere," Yusuf answered. "But none worth taking up. They were internal battles for the most part. Everyone was maneuvering to capture power within the vacuum created by the devastation of the war. I wasn't a player in those battles anymore, and their prospects seemed too bleak even if I had been."

"So whatever brought you to the States?" Pettis asked.

"Assassinations," Yusuf answered.

"Assassinations?" Pettis recoiled.

"Yes—of John F. Kennedy in 1963 and Malcolm X in 1965. Their deaths made big headlines in the Arab world. The United

States was not yet a vociferous ally of Israel, and I and my fellow Arabs looked to America with some bit of hope. I identified myself with the struggle of black Americans. Malcolm X, as a fellow believer in the Koran, intrigued me, and I knew a little about Martin Luther King. I was interested in the revolution that seemed to be taking place in America. With my own revolution in shambles, I began looking to the West. Less than a month after the war, I was making plans to go to the United States. I wanted to go to Harvard or Yale to get a degree."

"Ah," Lou said, "that better-than box of yours again."

Yusuf laughed. "Maybe so. On the other hand, they were the only American university names I really knew. A month later, having secured my papers, I boarded a plane in Amman to London and then on to New York City. From there, I made my way to New Haven, Connecticut, where Yale is located. I had to find a way to get accepted. If I couldn't get in there, then my plan was to move on to Boston, to Harvard.

"I had been in New Haven for less than a week when race riots broke out in August of 1967. I was there as well through the infamous Black Panther trials in 1970. It was also while there that I encountered the ideas that changed my view of myself, others, and the world. For it was there that I met a professor of philosophy, Benjamin Arrig, whose views began to change my own. I met Professor Arrig—or Ben, as he soon asked me to call him—on the New Haven Green as we watched black protesters being restrained by shield-carrying police who were shooting tear gas toward the crowds. The three Christian churches on the Green made for an interesting backdrop to the tension and violence. I ignored the warnings of the mounted policemen who told us to leave. The commotion, though substantial, was nothing compared to what I had grown accustomed to. I felt drawn to the spectacle.

"Just then I noticed a black man who seemed similarly drawn. He was among the onlookers, most of whom were white. I watched him curiously. Despite the combustible dangers of the moment, he remained stoically still—neither joining in anger nor running in fear. His face was serious with concern.

"I sidled up to him to get the black perspective on the conflict—a perspective that, as an oppressed Palestinian Arab, I thought I would readily understand. Here fought the equivalent of my Fatah brothers. Had I recognized any faces in the crowd, I probably would have thrown myself in the way of the canisters of gas. As I approached the man, I was looking to commiserate.

"'So the oppressed are fighting back,' I commented almost nonchalantly. My tone must have seemed oddly detached under the circumstances.

"'Yes,' the man responded, without moving his eyes from the scene, 'on both sides.'

"'Both sides?' I repeated in surprise.

"'Yes.'

"'How so?' I challenged. 'I only see tear gas on one side.'

"'If you look closely,' he answered, 'you will see the desire for tear gas on both sides.'

"I remember looking back at the boiling crowd and wondering what he meant, and how anyone could observe such desire even if it was there.

"'Where are you from?' he asked me, without taking his eyes off the scene.

"'Jerusalem, Palestine,' I answered.

"He didn't say anything.

"I turned back to the melee myself. 'I know what they are feeling,' I said, nodding toward the rioters.

"'Then I pity you,' the man said.

"I was taken aback.

"'Pity me? Why?'

"'Because you have become your own enemy,' he answered quietly but resolutely.

"'Because I want to fight back?' I objected. 'Because I want to right the wrongs that have been done to me and my people?'

"He didn't say anything.

"'What if circumstances are such that I'm justified in desiring tear gas?' I retorted, returning to his earlier comment.

"'Exactly,' he said.

"'Exactly?' I repeated in confusion. 'What is that supposed to mean?'

"'You have become your own enemy.'

"So began my education at the feet of Ben Arrig," Yusuf continued.

"What happened?" Lou asked.

"Over a period of three years, Ben completely laid waste to the assumptions I had taken to be the truth—to the personal biases I had believed to be reality. First, he taught me about the box, and then he taught me how you can and can't get out of it. Because of my deeply held biases against Jews, he spent a lot of time with me on the topic of racism and showed that it too was a feature of the box—of mine as much as anyone else's. 'If you see people of a particular race or culture as objects,' he told me, 'your view of them is racist, whatever your color or lack of color or your power or lack of power.' He showed me that this is the same for all divisions, whether between rich and poor, old and young, educated and uneducated, religious and nonreligious, Catholic and Protestant, Shia and Sunni.

"'When you begin to see others as people,' Ben told me, 'issues related to race, ethnicity, religion, and so on begin to look and feel different. You end up seeing people who have hopes, dreams, fears, and even justifications that resemble your own.'

"'But what if one group of people is oppressing another?' I once asked Ben.

"'Then the second group must be careful not to become oppressors themselves. A trap that is all too easy to fall into,' he added, 'when the justification of past abuse is readily at hand.'

"'How would they become oppressors themselves if they simply try to put an end to injustice?' I asked.

"'Because most who are trying to put an end to injustice only think of the injustices they believe they themselves have suffered. Which means that they are concerned not really with injustice but with themselves. They hide their focus on themselves behind the righteousness of their outward cause.'"

At this, Yusuf paused and looked around at the group. "Which brings me," he said, "back to Pettis's question of how we can ponder our situations anew."

"The people Ben and I witnessed that day on the New Haven Green appeared more concerned with their own burdens than with others'. I can't tell for sure as I wasn't in their skin, but it didn't appear that they were considering the burdens of those they were railing against, for example, or those whose lives they were putting in danger. It would have been well for them and their cause if they had begun to think as carefully about others as they did about themselves. If they had been able to find their way to an out-of-the-box place, they could have pondered their situations anew by asking a series of questions."

Walking to the board and beginning to write, he said, "Like these:"

- What are this person's or people's challenges, trials, burdens, and pains?
- How am I, or some group of which I am a part, adding to these challenges, trials, burdens, and pains?

- In what other ways have I or my group neglected or mistreated this person or group?
- In what ways are my better-than, I-deserve, worse-than, and must-be-seen-as boxes obscuring the truth about others and myself and interfering with potential solutions?
- What am I feeling I should do for this person or group? What could I do to help?

"With Ben's help," Yusuf said, as he turned back to the group, "I started to ask these questions—questions that helped me to ponder my situation anew. For most of my life I had been consumed with my own challenges, trials, burdens, and pains, and with those of my people. I had never thought to consider how the Israeli people might feel burdened as well, and how I might have added to the burdens they felt, and how I too had mistreated and neglected. As I began to ask these questions, the world began to change for me. I still saw my sufferings, but I was able to see the sufferings of others as well. And when seen in that light, my sufferings took on new meaning. They gave me a window into the pain that others might be feeling, some of it at my own hand. Since I no longer needed to feel justified, I no longer needed to sustain my own sufferings, and I could lay down my victimhood. I began to have feelings for and desires toward Israelis that I had before only faintly felt. I began to see possibilities—potential solutions to our problems that no one who is invested in the box can afford to see. I began to feel hope where before I felt only anger and despair.

"One quick story, if I might," he continued. "I went home to visit my mother a few years after my learning with Ben, and I made a point to visit someone else as well. *I wonder whatever happened to Mordechai Lavon?* I had thought. *Might he still be on the streets? Still begging? Still being ignored?*

"I walked up and down Bethlehem's Manger Street asking the merchants if they knew of an old blind man who begged nearby. He probably would have been seventy by then, I figured. No one seemed to know him or have any memory of him.

"Until finally I happened upon an old woman, herself a beggar. The few yellow teeth that remained jutted angularly from her mouth. Her dark leathery skin and deep wrinkles spoke of a lifetime on the street and under the sun.

"'Mordechai Lavon? Yes I knew him,' she cackled.

"'Do you know where I might find him?' I asked.

"'You won't,' she said, laughing oddly.

"'Why not?'

"'Died years ago. Right over there, 'round that corner.' She pointed a stubby finger across the street at an alleyway. 'Body lay there for three days, the police said. No one knew it until he started to smell. My, the smell! Whew!' she said, recoiling at the memory of it. 'He couldn't do much, old Mordechai, but he sure could stink!' And she cackled oddly again.

"I was surprised by how badly the news hurt me. *What a lonely life he led,* I lamented. *So many burdens, so many pains. And yet surrounded by others so focused only on their own pains that they never noticed his.* I turned to leave.

"'Hey Mister,' the woman called after me. "How 'bout some money?'

"I found myself stiffening my neck so as not to acknowledge her—not to feel her humanity. It was almost a reflex in me.

"*My, the box has staying power,* I thought, almost audibly. I stopped and took out my wallet. 'What's your name?' I asked.

"'Nahla,' she answered, 'Nahla Mahmuud.'

"I reached in and took out all the bills I was carrying.

"'For Mordechai,' I said, extending the bills to her.

"'Sure, Sir,' her face lit up. 'For Mordechai.'

Yusuf looked around at the group. By now each person was deep in thought and reflection.

Lou's mind was on three people in particular—Carol, Cory, and Kate. He felt a new desire awakening within him, a desire that built upon the thoughts he had had about Cory earlier that morning. He was feeling a desire to get to know his son. He felt an urge to begin writing a letter to him, to apologize, to share, and just to talk. He would have done so in that moment if he hadn't still been in the class. He resolved to write it that evening and to leave it here at Camp Moriah for the next mail run to the trail.

And Kate, he thought. *I'm so sorry for what I have done—for not listening, for stepping in and controlling how you ran your team, for my stupidity. What can I do to get you back? Yes, that is what I must do,* he resolved within, *I have to win you back.*

This thought led him to Carol—the woman whose heart he had "won" and then forgotten so many years before. He reached over and touched her hand. *I will not be forgetting again.* But then he realized how naïve this was. Of course he would. The box has staying power, just like Yusuf said. Lou knew he had much more to say to Carol than what he had managed to say that morning. A few good intentions would not overcome decades of bigheadedness. *Whatever she needs, I'll give her,* he told himself.

But you won't, came another voice from within. *You're going to go home and betroth yourself to your work again, and she'll again take up her role as convenient housemate and caretaker.*

No, I can't let that happen! Lou fairly shouted to himself. "What can I do to change things with my Mordechais before it's too late?" he asked urgently. "And how can I sustain that change?"

Yusuf smiled. "The ideas Ben Arrig taught me, in particular his liberating questions, will change everything if you can only find your way to an out-of-the-box place and ask them sincerely. Each time you find you're getting stuck, whether at work or in your family, you'll again have to find an out-of-the-box place just as we have found one together here, and then you'll have to get responsively curious once more. Your questions about others will break you free from your justifications and blame. For a while you will be able to see and feel clearly and to find a way forward that you hadn't before seen. That is what has happened to you here, is it not?"

Lou slowly nodded.

"Whether you stay free, however," Yusuf continued, "and to what extent you do, will depend on what happens next."

"Which is what?" Lou asked.

"The culminating step in the getting-out-of-the-box process."

21 · *Action*

Lou waited. "Okay, what is it?" he asked. "What is this final step you're talking about?"

"Gwyn," Yusuf said, "do you remember your dad's favorite word?"

"Too well, I'm afraid," she smirked.

"What does her father have to do with it?" Lou asked, impatiently.

"Actually, Lou, he has everything to do with it."

"How so?"

"Gwyn is Ben Arrig's daughter."

Lou wouldn't have been more surprised had the Easter Bunny come through the door. Jaw muscles went slack around the room.

"Don't be too impressed," Gwyn said in the silence of the gawking gazes, "Sometimes our parents are the last people we can hear, you know?" she said, mostly to herself.

Heads nodded everywhere.

"My ears have been closed to my dad's ideas for years. 'Don't try to feed your philosophy to me,' I used to tell him when he tried to suggest that I think of things a different way. He thought I should give up the hate I have for my former husband, forgive a sister who has wronged me, and rethink my opinions on race. But he was my dad. What did he know?"

She paused, and in the self-honesty of the moment, no one dared speak.

"I'm only here," she whispered, "because it was his dying wish that I come."

Lou broke the hush. "How long ago did he die?"

"Six months," she said. "Hit by a drunk driver as he crossed the street. He died the next morning."

"Oh, that's terrible," Carol said, "I can't imagine."

Elizabeth put her arm around Gwyn.

"So sorry, Gwyn," Miguel said.

"Yes," Ria agreed, shaking her head. "What a terrible tragedy."

"The irony has been almost too much to bear," Gwyn said. "Dad spent his life trying to help people let go of the grudges they carry about mistreatments they've received. And then he's killed by a drunk! His ideas couldn't save him from that."

"You're right, Gwyn," Yusuf agreed. "They couldn't. There is no way to avoid mistreatment altogether. That was never your father's point. There is, however, a way not to let your mistreatments destroy you and your peace. Even a mistreatment as hard to bear as this one must be."

Yusuf looked at her. "Do you want a break?"

She shook her head. "I'm fine." She then looked up at Yusuf and Avi. "Thanks for helping me to hear him," she said. "You've given me a lot to think about.

"Oh," she added after a moment, looking around at the rest of the group. "My father's favorite word was *action*."

"'Action'?" Lou repeated.

"Yes."

"Why?"

"I'm not entirely sure," she said. "But I bet Yusuf is."

"I think I know why, yes," he responded. "I think it was your father's way of reminding himself that although he could get out of the box by finding an out-of-the-box place and pondering the situation anew, in order to stay out and away from the box, he had to execute a strategy. That is, he had to *do* something."

"Do what?" Lou asked.

"Something only he would know," Yusuf answered.

Lou didn't like that answer at all. "But that can't help me then, can it? I'm sorry, Yusuf, but that's not good enough. I need more than that."

"You certainly do, Lou, but Ben was wise enough to know that what you need most is not something he or anyone else can give you. What you might think is not help enough is actually the only advice that can help at all. Anything else would be a lie."

"Then you need to tell me what you mean. I'm not following."

"Sure. Let me tie it back to some of the stories we have talked about together. Remember how Avi felt the desire to write a letter to Hamish?"

"Yes."

"He then acted on that desire, didn't he?"

Lou nodded.

"And do you remember how I felt the desire to find Mordechai?"

Lou nodded again.

"I then acted on that desire, just as Avi had acted on his, didn't I?"

"Yes," Lou said, still unsure where this was going.

"And Mei Li and Mike not only thought about taking off their shoes, they actually took them off.

"And remember Carol yesterday," he continued. "She voiced an apology to Miguel in front of the whole group, didn't she?"

"Yes," Lou said, in what turned out to be a whisper.

"She didn't only think about it, she actually did it."

Lou nodded.

Yusuf looked squarely at Lou. "I'm going to venture a guess about you, Lou. Do you mind?"

"Go ahead," Lou said, without any of the machismo that would have accompanied those words just twenty-four hours earlier.

"I'm going to guess that while we have been together, you too have had a number of desires awaken within—things you have felt the desire to do or begin doing for Cory or for Carol or perhaps for someone at work. Am I right?"

The desire to write Cory a letter came immediately to Lou's mind, and to apologize to Kate and do what he had to do to get her to come back to Zagrum. And of course his desire to be different toward Carol and the realization that he needed to figure out what to do to keep his boxes from poisoning their relationship.

"Yes, I have been feeling that," Lou answered.

"Then I want you to look again at the board," Yusuf said. "Once I recover a desire and sense toward people, where am I on this diagram?"

"At the top," Lou answered.

"So, out of the box, right?" Yusuf followed up.

"Yes, I guess that's right."

"The moment you've recovered a desire to help, you are out of the box toward the person. The question at that point is not how to get out of the box, it is rather how to stay out.

"Looking at the diagram from the top," he continued, "what do you need to do now to stay out of the box?"

THE CHOICE DIAGRAM

Sense/Desire

Help Mordechai by gathering his coins for him.
(I'm seeing Mordechai as a PERSON with needs, cares,
worries, and fears that matter, like mine do)

My Heart Is at Peace

|

CHOICE

Honor the sense   Betray the sense

↓   ↓

I continue to see   I begin to see Mordechai
Mordechai is a   in ways that justify
person like myself   my self-betrayal.
                                          He becomes an
                                       OBJECT of blame

My Heart Goes to War

View of Myself	**View of Mordechai**
Better than	No right to be there
A victim (so owed)	Robs me of peace
Bad (but made to be)	Zionist threat
Want to be seen well	Bigot
Feelings	**View of World**
Angry	Unfair
Depressed	Unjust
Bitter	Burdensome
Justified	Against me

Common Heart-at-War Styles
Better-Than
I-Deserve
Worse-Than   ⟶
Must-Be-Seen-As

"Honor the sense," Lou said, his mind turning.

"And who is the only person who will know the sense he must honor?" Yusuf asked.

Lou thought about that. "I guess only the person who is feeling it."

"Exactly," Yusuf replied. "And that is why I cannot tell you the precise thing you need to do. Only you, whose life it is—who knows the offenses, the missed opportunities, the petty unkindnesses, and so on—will know. I couldn't have told Avi that he needed to write a letter to Hamish, for example. Only he could have known that. Likewise, he may not have known enough about my life to suggest that I should seek out Mordechai Lavon. And notice, it is not just the sense of what to do but the *desire* to do it that's at issue. That desire has to come from within," he said. And then he added, "As it already has for you, Lou."

Yusuf paused. "When we have recovered those sensibilities toward others, we must then act on them. This is why *action* was Ben's favorite word. We need to honor the senses we have rather than betray them. If you, Lou, for example, were to betray the senses you are currently feeling toward others, you can be sure you would feel justified. You would then be right back in the box. So the key to staying out of the box once you have found your way out is to do what you're feeling you should do. It is to act on the out-of-the-box senses you are having."

At this, Yusuf added a fourth element to the board.

RECOVERING INNER CLARITY AND PEACE
(FOUR PARTS)

Getting out of the box
1. Look for the signs of the box (blame, justification, horribilization, common box styles, etc.).

2. Find an out-of-the-box place (out-of-the-box relationships, memories, activities, places, etc.).
3. Ponder the situation anew (i.e., from this out-of-the-box perspective). Ask
   - What are this person's or people's challenges, trials, burdens, and pains?
   - How am I, or some group of which I am a part, adding to these challenges, trials, burdens, and pains?
   - In what other ways have I or my group neglected or mistreated this person or group?
   - In what ways are my better-than, I-deserve, worse-than, and must-be-seen-as boxes obscuring the truth about others and myself and interfering with potential solutions?
   - What am I feeling I should do for this person or group? What could I do to help?

Staying out of the box

4. Act upon what I have discovered; do what I am feeling I should do.

"This, then," Yusuf said, "is how peace can be recovered inwardly, even when we are surrounded by war. We stay on the lookout for signs of the box. We then find an out-of-the-box place from where we can ponder the situation with more clarity. And then we begin to consider others' burdens instead of just our own. In the course of this, we'll typically see things that we haven't seen before and feel moved, therefore, to take certain new actions. In the moment we recover this sense or desire to help, we have found our way out of the box. Whether we *stay* out and retain a heart at peace will depend on whether we honor that sense or desire."

"But what about the wars around us?" Lou asked. "They won't be solved simply by finding peace within, as important as that might be."

Yusuf smiled. "That depends."

"On what?" Lou asked.

"On the nature of the conflict," Yusuf answered. "In conflicts simply between you and another, I think you'd be surprised by how fully a solution to the inner war solves the outer war as well." His eyes lingered on Lou. "Think about you and Gwyn, for example, Lou. There were times yesterday when you almost got out of your chairs and started duking it out. But look at you now."

They looked at each other. Lou faked a left hook, and everyone laughed.

"But how about other kinds of conflicts?" Pettis asked. "Conflicts with more history to them, for example, or conflicts between many people. A single heart at peace won't necessarily solve those."

"No, you're right, Pettis. It won't. But notice what it *will* do. Being out of the box will allow you for the first time to see the situation clearly, without exaggeration or justification. It will position you to begin to exert influence toward peace instead of provocation toward war. While you are correct that a heart at peace alone won't solve your complex outer problems, those problems can't begin to be solved without it."

"Then what else?" Elizabeth asked. "Yesterday you said we would end up with a strategy for helping others to change. I assume changing myself in the way you've shown us is the necessary first step. But what then?"

"Then you work to help things go right," Yusuf answered.

"How?"

"By doing what we have been doing with you."

PART IV

Spreading Peace

22 · A Strategy of Peace

"Do you remember yesterday morning when I drew a pyramid and divided it into two levels?" Yusuf asked. "I called one level 'dealing with things that are going wrong,' and the deeper level 'helping things go right.' Remember?"

Everyone nodded.

"Then you'll remember how we agreed that we normally spend most of our time dealing with things that are going wrong, even though that isn't ideal."

Again, the group nodded.

"I'd like to give you more detail around that pyramid," he said. "It forms a structure that governs everything we do here at Camp Moriah with the children, with the staff, and with you. It shows not only how to *find* peace, but how to *make* it. It shows how to replace conflict with cooperation. Yesterday we called it the Change Pyramid because it guides all attempts to get others to change or improve. Since the change we at Camp Moriah are most interested in is the change from war to peace—first within us, and then without—we often call the more detailed version the Peacemaking Pyramid."

At that, Yusuf turned and drew a pyramid similar to the one he had drawn the day before. As before, he divided it between dealing with things that are going wrong and helping things go right. But then he divided it still further into six levels and wrote "Correct" in the top level.

THE PEACEMAKING PYRAMID

Turning back to the group, he said, "When we're trying to effect change in others, whether in a child, in a team at work, or in a region of the world, we are trying to correct them, are we not? We are believing that circumstances would be better if another changed. Right?"

"Yes," they all answered.

"But that's wrong, isn't it?" Ria asked. "Thinking that others need to change is already a problem. Right?"

Yusuf smiled. "Do you think it's a problem that you want your boy to change?" Yusuf asked Ria.

She frowned. "No, not really," she said.

"If he doesn't," Miguel grunted, "his life'll be a mess."

Yusuf nodded. "So it isn't as simple as saying that wanting others to change is a problem, is it?" he asked.

"I guess not," Ria answered, suddenly unsure of her understanding.

"What would be a problem," Yusuf continued, "is to insist that others need to change while being unwilling to consider how we ourselves might need to change too. *That* would be a problem."

"Right," Pettis agreed, "because you wouldn't be able to invite others to change if you were in that kind of box yourself. You'd only invite them to war with you."

"Yes," Yusuf agreed. "And for one additional reason as well: To the extent I'm in the box toward others, my beliefs about their need to change might actually be mistaken. Maybe my spouse isn't as unreasonable as I've been thinking, for example. Or maybe I've been overreacting toward my child. Or maybe the other team at work actually has some things right. I won't be able to tell the difference between what changes would be helpful and what changes would simply be helpful to my box until I get out of the box.

"As we've discovered together over the last two days," Yusuf continued, "the most important part of helping things go right is getting out of the box ourselves." At that, Yusuf turned back to the board and wrote, "Get out of the box/Obtain a heart at peace" in the lowest level of the pyramid.

THE PEACEMAKING PYRAMID

Correct

Dealing with things that are going wrong

Helping things go right

Get out of the box/
Obtain a heart at peace

"For our purposes here," he continued, "this is also the biggest thing that has been going wrong in each of our families. Our hearts have been too often at war toward our children and toward each other. So everything we've done together has been with the purpose of trying to correct that. And everything we've done to invite that change is detailed by these middle levels of the Peacemaking Pyramid."

"But they're blank," Lou objected, only half in jest.

"Let's fill them in by considering an example, Lou," Yusuf smiled. "Let's say, for example, that you needed to change something about yourself."

"Purely hypothetical," Lou cracked. "I understand."

"Yes," Yusuf smiled again. "Let's suppose when you came in and sat down yesterday morning that Avi had said to you, 'Lou, you need to get out of the box!' Do you think that would have helped much?"

"Well I think he did just about say that to me," Lou laughed. Avi busted into a big smile at that as well. "But no, alone that wouldn't have done much good."

"What if when you refused, he punished you? Maybe he could have sent you to another room until you wised up, for example. Or maybe he could have withheld water or refreshment privileges from you. Do you think that would have helped you out of the box?"

"Uh, no," Lou said matter-of-factly.

"So you can see that correction alone rarely gets others to change," Yusuf said. "It will help if I'm out of the box myself when I'm correcting, but even then it usually isn't enough. So what else might help? The pyramid suggests four categories of action that when combined with a heart at peace create a strong invitation to change and peace.

"The first of these is what we have been doing during much of the last two days: we have been teaching."

At this, Yusuf added "Teach & Communicate" to the level below "Correct" on the pyramid.

THE PEACEMAKING PYRAMID

"It is no help to tell you to get out of the box," Yusuf continued, "if you don't even know what the box is. Likewise, any correction at work will be for naught if the people I am trying to correct lack the information they need to perform their jobs. It is the same in the realm of world events. If a country doesn't clearly and persuasively communicate the reasons for actions it is taking in the world community, it invites resistance to those efforts. Whatever the context, if I am failing in my teaching, my correction will likely fail as well.

"Going deeper," Yusuf continued, "it is no good trying to teach if I myself am not listening and learning. We've had some ideas to teach you while we are together, of course, but it wouldn't have helped much if we ignored your issues and questions and simply taught according to our plan."

At this, Yusuf added "Listen & Learn" to the next level of the pyramid.

THE PEACEMAKING PYRAMID

Yusuf turned to face the group again. "We've been trying to listen to you all the way along," he said, "and to speak to the issues you have been concerned about. Yesterday, I think I must not have been doing that very well, as you'll remember that Lou thought I was ducking his questions."

"Actually, I think it was more a case of him ducking your answers," Elizabeth joked.

"Touché, Elizabeth," Lou laughed. "Touché."

Yusuf smiled as well. "This attempt to learn from you," he continued, "actually goes back to well before you came here yesterday. Remember how we had you write to us about your children?"

Most in the room nodded.

"That was as much to learn about you as to learn about them. Avi and I have been thinking about you for months and have tried to organize our teaching in light of what we've learned."

"On the subject of learning," Avi jumped in, "another important function of the learning level of the pyramid is that it keeps reminding us that we might be mistaken in our views and opinions. Maybe an objective I've been insisting upon at work is unwise, for example. Or maybe a strategy I've been taking with my child is hurtful. Or maybe the lesson structure we had planned isn't working, and so on. The learning level of the pyramid keeps inviting us toward humility. It reminds us that the person or group we wish would change may not be the only one who needs to change! It continually invites us to hone our views and opinions."

"All of which applies as well to world events," Yusuf agreed. "How effective will a country's communications be if its leaders are not actively trying to learn about and from the people they are trying to communicate with? If we want change in the Middle East, for example, but remain ignorant about the people there and their thoughts and opinions, how effective will our teaching be? And if we are sure about others' need to change but are unwilling to let what we learn from them inform changes in us as well, how much change are we likely to invite? If we are poor learners, our teaching will be ineffective. Failure at one level of the pyramid always undermines success at each of the levels above it.

"Which leaves us," he continued, pointing to the diagram, "with two more levels to consider. What do you suppose might undercut my willingness or ability to learn from others and therefore the effectiveness of my teaching?"

No one responded immediately.

"How about this?" he asked, writing "Build the relationship" in the next level of the pyramid.

THE PEACEMAKING PYRAMID

"What if my relationship with the people who work for me, for example, is poor?" he continued. "What impact do you think that might have on my ability to learn from them and the effectiveness of my teaching?"

Lou's mind went immediately to John Rencher. It was clear to Lou that his poor personal relationship with Rencher made all of Lou's work with the union more difficult.

"Or how about your relationship with the child you brought to us?" Yusuf continued. "Would you say it is strong and healthy?"

Shoulders slumped around the room.

"If not, I would wager that there is much you don't know about your child, much that he has not shared with you. Your learning has been stunted as a result, and your efforts to teach and correct have therefore been undercut as well. Perhaps what you need to do is figure out how to build your relationship with your child. Put his problems aside for a moment. What does he like to do? Could you spend time doing it with him? What actions could you take to help build the relationship?"

Lou sat in memory. He and Cory had not had a heart-to-heart for years. They used to golf together, too long ago. He didn't know what Cory wanted in life anymore, what he hoped for, or who he dreamed to be. Lou wasn't even sure how Cory liked to spend his time. He just knew that no son of his was going to have a drug problem! Lou's correction and teaching of Cory ever since had had little effect. And now he knew at least two reasons why: he had been too sure of himself to bother learning from and about Cory, and he had completely abandoned efforts to build their relationship. Everything between them the last couple of years had revolved around Cory's drug problem. It was the subtext beneath every word between them—spoken and unspoken.

Lou shook his head. "How pathetic," he said.

"What?" Yusuf asked. "What's pathetic?"

"How I've been," Lou answered. "It's so obvious I should have been spending time trying to build my relationship with Cory, but that thought hasn't even crossed my mind lately. It's like the box has blinded me or something."

"That's not far off," Yusuf said. "Think about it: if I'm sure I'm right, there is little hope of seeing where I am failing. So I keep trying the same old things—the same lectures, for example, and the same punishments. And I keep getting the same outcomes: others with problems. On the one hand, I hate it, but on the other hand, I get my justification, which is what I most want when I'm in the box. My need for justification blinds me to all kinds of possibilities. Even to the obvious ones."

Lou shook his head in disgust.

"What's in the last space?" Pettis asked. "Between Build the relationship and Get out of the box?"

"You are," Yusuf answered. "After a fashion anyway. When we at Camp Moriah are thinking about your children, you occupy the next space. That's because this level of the pyramid is about building relationships with others who have influence with the person or group we are trying to help. You have the biggest influence in your children's lives, so if we want to be a positive influence with your children we better have strong relationships with you. The pyramid reminds parents of the same thing—that they must build relationships with those who have influence with their children, beginning with their spouse. Or former spouse, for that matter."

"How about with their friends?" Ria asked. "Are you saying we need to build relationships with them?"

"I hope that's not what you're saying," Pettis spoke up. "I don't want my daughter to have some of her relationships. That's been part of the problem. I want her to pull away from them."

"Has your detached denouncement of those friends invited your daughter to pull away?" Yusuf asked.

Pettis hesitated. "Not really, no."

"Then you might think about applying the pyramid to your situation," Yusuf said. "Let's take a look at the overall structure."

THE PEACEMAKING PYRAMID

Looking at Pettis, Yusuf continued. "I take it you've been trying to correct your daughter's choice of friends—maybe by talking her friends down, for example, or by limiting her ability to be with them."

Pettis nodded slightly.

"My guess is that although you've tried to talk with her about this, the communication hasn't gone very well."

"That's mostly true, yes," Pettis admitted.

"If so, the pyramid invites us to think deeper," Yusuf responded. "The next level deeper invites you to consider how well you have been listening to and learning from your daughter. Do you know what she likes in those friends, for example? Do you know what her interests are and why she has therefore chosen the friends she has? Do you know what struggles she is having? Do you know, for example, how your divorce has affected her?"

This revelation surprised Lou. He'd hardly even noted that Pettis was alone. He looked at the learning level of the pyramid. *Maybe I don't care enough about others to be curious about them*, he wondered. The thought weighed on him.

"Or going deeper still," Yusuf continued, "how strong is your relationship with your daughter? The healthier the relationship, the more likely she would be to consider your opinions about her friends. Have you been spending ample time with her to build the relationship?

"And then, finally, how about your relationships with others who have influence with her? With her mother, for example, and with her friends."

Lou looked at Pettis, who seemed to be struggling.

"You know," Yusuf continued, "I learned something interesting with one of my own boys. He had a friend I didn't like either. Not one bit. I tried all the standard father strategies. I talked badly about the boy, kept my son from seeing him, and so on."

Pettis looked up from his troubles at Yusuf.

"That's why I could guess what you had tried as well," Yusuf smiled. "When I was complaining about it to Avi one day, he told me that I should begin practicing what I teach! With that nudge, I began to apply the pyramid to the situation. In my case, my son didn't begin losing interest in his friend until I started inviting the friend over to our house. And by then, I'd actually started to like the kid. I was almost sorry to see him go. Until I got out of the box toward my son, my efforts to separate him from his friends only made him want them all the more."

Yusuf looked at Pettis, who appeared deep in thought. "The old saying 'The enemy of my enemy is my friend,'" Yusuf began, "is the arithmetic of the box. Subtract the box from that equation and you and your daughter may discover new answers.

"In fact," he continued, looking around at the rest, "we'll *all* discover new answers. If we apply it, the Peacemaking Pyramid will guide us in all our interactions—in our homes, in our workplaces, and in the world. It will suggest actions to take while keeping our minds and hearts clear. It will help us improve our influence for good in every context, even the most difficult ones.

"That is," he continued, "if we remember to apply the pyramid's important lessons."

23 · *Lessons*

"Lessons?" Lou asked.

"Yes," Yusuf answered. "The pyramid illuminates three main lessons—axioms that guide its application in all situations. We've already mentioned the first."

At this, he wrote the following.

LESSON 1
Most time and effort should be spent at the lower
levels of the pyramid.

"Remember: we want to spend most of our time in the levels of the pyramid below correction, which is exactly the opposite of what we normally do. We want to spend most of our time actively helping things go right rather than dealing with things that are going wrong. We want to get out of the box, build relationships, listen and learn, teach and communicate. Where circumstances are such that we choose to engage in correction of some kind—whether by putting a little child on time-out or by sending war planes into the skies above a country that has attacked us—the lower levels of the pyramid become even more important. Correction is by nature provocational. So where we choose to correct, we need to increase our efforts at the lower levels of the pyramid all the more. If we believe military force is necessary, for example, then we would be wise to increase our communicating, learning, and relationship-building efforts even more.

"When we actively live these lower levels of the pyramid, we normally discover that we need to spend less time on correction than we have in the past. We also discover that when we need to impose correction, it is more likely to have an impact than it did in the past because our correction will grow out of an ongoing effort and context. It will no longer seem capricious or arbitrary but will feel connected to our deeper efforts to help things go right. Whether at home, at work, or among nations in the world, lesson number one of the Peacemaking Pyramid is that most time and effort should be spent at the lower levels of the pyramid.

"Now for lesson two," he continued.

LESSON 2
The solution to a problem at one level of the pyramid is always below that level of the pyramid.

"This lesson also runs counter to our normal reflex. When our correction isn't working, we normally bear down harder and correct more. And when our teaching is going poorly, we often try to rescue it by talking more and insisting more. That is, we drone on in an attempt to correct the problems we have created by droning on!"

Lou thought of all his "teaching" sessions with Cory.

"If I am correcting and correcting but problems remain," Yusuf continued, "that is a clue that the solution to the problem I am facing will not be found in further correction. Likewise with teaching. And if I learn and learn, even going so far as to revise my opinions, but problems persist, perhaps what I need to do is go out and engage with others personally. Maybe I need to increase my efforts to build relationships both with those I am dealing with and with others who deal with them.

"Mei Li shared with us one of the key ways we build relationships here at Camp Moriah: in all that we do with others, we try to 'take off our shoes' with them. We join them in the limitations they face and hold ourselves to the same requirements. For example, the lunchtime assignment we gave you yesterday—to see everyone during that time as a person—was an assignment Avi and I took upon ourselves as well. And we pondered the conflicts and boxes in our own lives last night, just as we asked you to do. And just as you have had impressions during our time together of things you need to do for someone, we too have had the same impressions and will leave today with the same commitment that you will have: to do what we're feeling we should do to help things go right.

"If I find I have trouble building relationships despite my efforts to do so, this second lesson suggests that a solution, if there is to be one, will not be found simply by spending more time with others. I might have a problem at the lowest level of the pyramid—in my way of being.

"Which brings us," Yusuf said, "to the pyramid's lowest level, and to its third lesson."

LESSON 3
Ultimately, my effectiveness at each level of the pyramid depends on the deepest level of the pyramid— my way of being.

"I can put all the effort I want into trying to build my relationships," Yusuf said, "but if I'm in the box while I'm doing it, it won't help much. If I'm in the box while I'm trying to learn, I'll only end up hearing what I want to hear. And if I'm in the box while I'm trying to teach, I'll invite resistance in all who listen."

Yusuf looked around at the group. "My effectiveness in everything above the lowest level of the pyramid depends on the lowest level. My question for you is why?"

Everyone looked at the pyramid.

"You might try looking at the way-of-being diagram from yesterday," Yusuf said.

"I get it," Lou said after a moment.

"What?" Yusuf asked. "What are you seeing?"

"Well, the way-of-being diagram tells us that almost any outward behavior can be done in either of two ways—with a heart that's at war or a heart that's at peace."

"Yes," Yusuf agreed. "And what does that have to do with the Peacemaking Pyramid?"

"Everything above the lowest level of the pyramid is a behavior," Lou answered.

"Exactly," Yusuf said. "So anything I do to build relationships, to learn, to teach, or to correct can be done either in the box or out. And as we learned yesterday from the collusion diagram, when I act from within the box, I invite resistance. Although there are two ways to invade Jerusalem, only one of those ways invites cooperation. The other sows the seeds of its own failure. So while the pyramid tells us where to look and what kinds of things to do in order to invite change in others, this last lesson reminds us that it cannot be faked. The pyramid keeps helping me to remember that I might be the problem and giving me hints of how I might begin to become part of a solution. A culture of change can never be created by behavioral strategy alone. Peace—whether at home, work, or between peoples—is invited only when an intelligent outward strategy is married to a peaceful inward one.

"This is why we have spent most of our time together working to improve ourselves at this deepest level. If we don't get our hearts right, our strategies won't much matter. Once we get our hearts right, however, outward strategies matter a lot. The virtue of the pyramid is that it reminds us of the essential foundation—change in ourselves—while also revealing a behavioral strategy for inviting change in others. It reminds us to get out of the box ourselves at the same time that it tells us how to invite others to get out as well."

As Lou listened, he saw how the pyramid could help him at Zagrum. First of all, he needed Kate back. He hadn't known where to begin, but now he knew that he needed to talk with her—teach her about what he had discovered about himself and tell her about the changes he was committed to making. And he knew as well that he had to ask her to help him see where he was still blind. He needed to learn from her, and he was finally willing to. As for the relationship, he wasn't sure he could repair it, given how he'd acted. But he suddenly knew where he had to begin. He had removed a ladder she was using as a prop for her team because he thought it was a stupid idea. His taking the ladder was symbolic of much that was wrong about his style with people, just as Kate had said. As silly as it sounded, he knew he needed to take her a ladder. He resolved that he would take it to her home in Litchfield, Connecticut, as soon as he and Carol returned home.

Which brought him to Carol. He knew that he tended toward better-than and I-deserve boxes and that others often faded away into the scenery as a result. He was afraid of that happening again, especially toward Carol. It occurred to him that the pyramid could help with this. If he could keep reminding himself to work the lower levels of the pyramid, he would remember to stay in the middle of learning from Carol—to wonder about her day, for example, and her feelings. It would also help him to remember to keep working to build their relationship—

to spend time together doing what she enjoys, for example. And at the bottom level of the pyramid, he knew it would help if he could find ways to keep remembering how Carol was the one who had held their family together, often despite him. If he could keep remembering that, it would be much harder to start thinking that he was somehow superior or more important.

Lou looked at the pyramid again. He finally had some hope. But he was still worried. "I'm worried that I'm going to blow it," he confided aloud.

"Of course you will!" Yusuf laughed. "Of course you're going to blow it. We all will. You're a person, after all, not an automaton. If the possibility of failure paralyzes you, you might wonder what box is demanding that you be perfect."

"You're saying I have a need to be perfect?"

"It might be worth considering. Must-be-seen-as boxes can wield paralyzing impact."

Lou chuckled.

"What's so funny?" Yusuf asked.

"I keep telling myself I don't really have any must-be-seen-as issues, but they keep popping up."

"Most of us justify ourselves in all of the basic ways to one degree or another," Yusuf said. "At least I know I do."

At that, Yusuf looked around at everyone—at Lou, Carol, Elizabeth, Gwyn, Pettis, Miguel, Ria, Teri, and Carl. "Regretfully, at least for me," he added with a smile, "our time together is about finished. I appreciate the time and effort you have devoted to this. You have been pondering your lives in bold ways. I hope you will be both troubled and inspired as a result; troubled because you know that the box is always just a choice away but hopeful for the very same reason because freedom from the box is also just a choice away—a choice that is available to us in every moment.

"May I mention one more thing to you before we go our separate ways today?" he asked.

"Please," everyone answered.

"I want to share with you why we chose to name our program Camp Moriah."

24 · *Peace on Mount Moriah*

"As we mentioned earlier," Yusuf began, "Mount Moriah is the hill in Jerusalem that is graced by the Muslim shrine known as the Dome of the Rock. This real estate is no doubt the most religiously revered in the world. It is valued by Muslims as one of their holiest sites, remembered by Jews and Christians alike as the site of the Holy Temple in ancient times, and looked to by some as the site at which another temple will one day be built. The eyes and hearts of the world are focused on Mount Moriah.

"Because of this, that revered piece of land is an outward symbol both of our conflicts and our possibilities. One side may say it is their holy place, set apart for millennia. Others may believe it was bequeathed them by God. There seems to be little opportunity for peace in such views. Looked at in another way, however, this passionate belief provides the portal to peace, for only one who cherishes and reveres something can understand what it means to others who regard it the same way.

"From within the box, passions, beliefs, and personal needs seem to divide us. When we get out of the box, however, we learn that this has been a lie. Our passions, beliefs, and needs do not divide but unite: it is by *virtue* of our own passions, beliefs, and needs that we can see and understand others'. If we have beliefs we cherish, then we know how important others' beliefs must be to them. And if we have needs, then our own experience equips us to notice the needs of others. To scale

Mount Moriah is to ascend a mountain of hope. At least it is if one climbs in a way that lifts his soul to an out-of-the-box summit—a place from where he sees not only buildings and homes but people as well.

"And so, a land stands divided. And within that land, a meaning-filled hill stands as a symbol both of the divide and of the hope for overcoming it.

"Our homes and workplaces are divided as well. Within each rise our own Mount Moriahs—outward issues that come to symbolize all of the inner turmoil we are feeling. In one home it might be the dishes, in another the finances, and in yet another the disciplining of the children. At work, we may come to focus on the title or the status or the level of respect we think we deserve. We begin to do battle around these issues, and the more we battle, the larger they loom on the landscape until finally our home and workplace quakes build mountains so high they create their own weather systems. If you don't believe me, just witness what happens to the climate in a room when parties start doing battle around one of their Mount Moriahs.

"The issue, of course, is not the mountain, whether that mountain is the dishes or the lawn or the title; or whether, for that matter, the mountain is Mount Moriah itself. No, the issue lies *beneath* the mountain in the realities in our hearts that make these mountains our battlegrounds.

"Lasting solutions to our outward conflicts are possible only to the extent that we find real solutions to our inner ones. An uneasy détente may be possible in Israel by focusing only on the surface of things—on economics, for example, or on security. But lasting peace will not be. The same can be said for our homes and workplaces."

"But détente *is* preferable to bloodshed," Gwyn said.

"It certainly is," Yusuf agreed. "But let's not fool ourselves. Cool détente, while preferable today, is still a war waiting for tomorrow. Lasting solutions to the battles in our workplaces, homes, and battlefields will come only as we end the war in our souls. We end that war first by finding and extending our out-of-the-box places. And we help others out of their inner wars by being for them an out-of-the-box place ourselves—the way Ben was for me, the way Hamish was for Avi, the way Mei Li and Mike were for Jenny, and the way all of you have become for one another. We have begun living the pyramid together, which is why our feelings today are so much more peaceful than they were yesterday morning."

The group looked around at each other.

"My friends," Yusuf said, "Avi and I and the team here promise that we will strive to be that kind of place for your children. We will take off our shoes toward them, hoping to create a space that invites them to ponder their lives anew and make changes they would do well to make. We invite you to do the same, whatever that might mean for you."

Lou looked to the day, sixty days in the future, when he would once again see his boy—shoeless, he hoped, if he could maintain what he had learned until then. In the meantime, he had some letters to write.

"But what if my boy still does drugs?" Miguel asked. "What if this program doesn't fix him?"

"Then he will be lucky to have a father like you, Miguel, who will strive to love him all the same."

"But I don't want him on drugs!"

"No. Of course you don't. Which is why you won't stop trying to help him, no matter how long it takes. Even if he doesn't like it.

"Don't misunderstand," Yusuf added. "Despite our best efforts, we may find that some battles are unavoidable. Some around us will inevitably choose war. May we in those cases remember Saladin and remember that while certain outward battles may need to be fought, they can nevertheless be fought with hearts that are at peace.

"And," he said as he looked appreciatively around the room, "may we remember the deeper lesson as well: that your, and my, and the world's hoped-for outward peace depends most fully not on the peace we seek or the wars we wage without but on the peace we establish within.

"Which should bring you hope," he added. "It means that however bleak things look on the outside, the peace that starts it all, the peace within, is merely a choice away. A choice that changes everything. You already know this, as you are already beginning to feel differently about your children.

"If we can find our way to peace toward children who have stolen from us, spouses who have mistreated us, and even drunks who have taken our fathers from us," he said, glancing at Gwyn, "what mountains are too high for human hearts to scale?

"Your spouse, your children, your colleagues, your enemies— may you choose to see them all as people, and may you therefore discover solutions you've never known and summits you can enjoy together."

Index

About The Arbinger Institute

Arbinger is a worldwide institute that helps organizations, families, individuals, and communities to solve the problems that have been created by the little-known but pervasive problem of self-deception (the problem of not knowing and resisting the possibility that one has a problem). Most conflicts are perpetuated by the problem of self-deception, as are most failures in communication and most breakdowns in trust and accountability. Unless one can solve the problem of not knowing one has a problem, these other problems necessarily remain.

Try telling someone he or she has a problem, however, and the depth of the problem of self-deception becomes clear. How can you help someone to see something he or she is unwilling to see? This is the central challenge created by the problem of self-deception and the challenge that Arbinger's work is designed to overcome.

Arbinger's materials educate people about the problem of self-deception, and Arbinger's methodologies help people to overcome it. In the words of an early reviewer of *The Anatomy of Peace*, "Arbinger helps people to see in a different way—to see problems differently, conflicts differently, challenges differently, opportunities differently, each other differently." To which another added, "I know of no tool or way of thinking that contributes so masterfully to real, lasting peace—in families, organizations, communities, and nations."

Arbinger's ideas resulted from a decades-long exploration by an international team of scholars into the problem of self-deception. The new understanding that emerged gradually began to seep into the public consciousness. By the early 1990s Arbinger was formed to introduce these discoveries to individuals and organizations around the world.

Arbinger's first book, *Leadership and Self-Deception*, published in the year 2000, quickly became an international bestseller. Launched with no fanfare when Arbinger (and its work) was little known, the book generated tremendous word-of-mouth momentum. Sales of the book continue to grow at an increasing rate even today. The book is currently available in nearly twenty languages.

Since *Leadership and Self-Deception* was published, many readers have clamored for a book that explores Arbinger's work more deeply and that applies that work more explicitly to issues outside the workplace as well as within. *The Anatomy of Peace* was written for this purpose and out of the desire to help resolve conflicts large and small that burden families, workplaces, and communities.

Arbinger is composed of people who have been trained in business, law, economics, philosophy, the family, education, coaching, and psychology. They come from diverse cultural backgrounds and from all religious and nonreligious traditions and belief systems. What they share is a deep understanding and passion for the ideas underlying Arbinger's work—a compelling model of human understanding that offers people a common language with which to talk about and settle their differences, whatever their cultures, races, classes, religions, and beliefs.

The members of Arbinger are mobilized in four directions—to help (1) organizations, (2) communities, (3) individuals and families, and (4) those in the helping professions. In support of these groups, Arbinger offers public courses, consulting and coaching services, and tailored organizational interventions (including train-the-trainer options). Arbinger's clients range from individuals who are seeking help in their lives to many of the largest companies and governmental institutions in the world.

Headquartered in the United States, Arbinger now has operations in many countries, including the United Kingdom, France, Germany, the Netherlands, Israel, India, Singapore, Australia, Taiwan, Korea, Japan, Mexico, Canada, and Bermuda. Arbinger is led internationally by Jim Ferrell, Duane Boyce, Paul Smith, and Terry Warner. Local managing directors guide Arbinger's work in territories around the world.

For more information about Arbinger's public workshops, family and organizational services, individual coaching, and other inquiries, please call Arbinger's worldwide headquarters at 1-801-292-3131 or visit Arbinger on the Web at http://www.arbinger.com.

Introducing the international word-of-mouth phenomenon that started it all

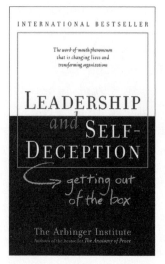

Written before *The Anatomy of Peace* but set years later, this powerful book tells the story of Tom Callum, a young executive applying for a position at Zagrum Company–Lou Herbert's company. Lou has transformed Zagrum using the ideas he learned at Camp Moriah, and in *Leadership and Self-Deception*, Tom learns from Lou and others how these concepts can not only change lives but also be applied to create healthy, humane, and productive workplaces.

Over a half million copies sold! Published in over 20 languages!

Available from your favorite bookseller, from Arbinger, or from Berrett-Koehler. To read a free excerpt or to discuss the book, go to www.arbinger.com.

ISBN 978-1-57675-174-9

BK

Berrett–Koehler Publishers, Inc.
San Francisco
www.bkconnection.com

Berrett–Koehler
Publishers

Berrett-Koehler is an independent publisher dedicated to an ambitious mission: *Creating a World That Works for All*.

We believe that to truly create a better world, action is needed at all levels—individual, organizational, and societal. At the individual level, our publications help people align their lives with their values and with their aspirations for a better world. At the organizational level, our publications promote progressive leadership and management practices, socially responsible approaches to business, and humane and effective organizations. At the societal level, our publications advance social and economic justice, shared prosperity, sustainability, and new solutions to national and global issues.

A major theme of our publications is "Opening Up New Space." Berrett-Koehler titles challenge conventional thinking, introduce new ideas, and foster positive change. Their common quest is changing the underlying beliefs, mindsets, institutions, and structures that keep generating the same cycles of problems, no matter who our leaders are or what improvement programs we adopt.

We strive to practice what we preach—to operate our publishing company in line with the ideas in our books. At the core of our approach is stewardship, which we define as a deep sense of responsibility to administer the company for the benefit of all of our "stakeholder" groups: authors, customers, employees, investors, service providers, and the communities and environment around us.

We are grateful to the thousands of readers, authors, and other friends of the company who consider themselves to be part of the "BK Community." We hope that you, too, will join us in our mission.

A BK Life Book

This book is part of our BK Life series. BK Life books change people's lives. They help individuals improve their lives in ways that are beneficial for the families, organizations, communities, nations, and world in which they live and work. To find out more, visit **www.bk-life.com**.

Berrett–Koehler
Publishers

A community dedicated to creating
a world that works for all

Visit Our Website: www.bkconnection.com

Read book excerpts, see author videos and Internet movies, read
our authors' blogs, join discussion groups, download book apps, find
out about the BK Affiliate Network, browse subject-area libraries of
books, get special discounts, and more!

Subscribe to Our Free E-Newsletter, the *BK Communiqué*

Be the first to hear about new publications, special discount offers,
exclusive articles, news about bestsellers, and more! Get on the list
for our free e-newsletter by going to **www.bkconnection.com**.

Get Quantity Discounts

Berrett-Koehler books are available at quantity discounts for orders
of ten or more copies. Please call us toll-free at (800) 929-2929 or
email us at **bkp.orders@aidcvt.com**.

Join the BK Community

BKcommunity.com is a virtual meeting place where people from
around the world can engage with kindred spirits to create a world
that works for all. **BKcommunity.com** members may create their own
profiles, blog, start and participate in forums and discussion groups,
post photos and videos, answer surveys, announce and register for
upcoming events, and chat with others online in real time. Please join
the conversation!